# Helping Your Anxious Teen

A Practical Guide for Parents To Help Your Child Learn To Manage Everyday Anxiety

Katherine Guzman

© **Copyright 2021 - All rights reserved.**

The content contained within this book may not be reproduced, duplicated or transmitted without direct written permission from the author or the publisher.

Under no circumstances will any blame or legal responsibility be held against the publisher, or author, for any damages, reparation, or monetary loss due to the information contained within this book, either directly or indirectly.

**Legal Notice:**

This book is copyright protected. It is only for personal use. You cannot amend, distribute, sell, use, quote or paraphrase any part, or the content within this book, without the consent of the author or publisher.

**Disclaimer Notice:**

Please note the information contained within this document is for educational and entertainment purposes only. All effort has been executed to present accurate, up to date, reliable, complete information. No warranties of any kind are declared or implied. Readers acknowledge that the author is not engaging in the rendering of legal, financial, medical or professional advice. The content within this book has been derived from various sources. Please consult a licensed professional before attempting any techniques outlined in this book.

By reading this document, the reader agrees that under no circumstances is the author responsible for any losses, direct or indirect, that are incurred as a result of the use of information contained within this document, including, but not limited to, errors, omissions, or inaccuracies.

# TABLE OF CONTENTS

Introduction ............................................................................. 7

**Chapter 1: Understanding Anxiety** ........................................... 11

*What is Anxiety?* ........................................................................ 12

*What Causes Anxiety?* .............................................................. 13

*Types of Anxiety Disorders* ...................................................... 15

*Common Signs of Anxiety* ........................................................ 18

*Difference Between Anxiety and Fear* ..................................... 21

**Chapter 2: Teens and Anxiety** ................................................... 23

*Is Teenage Anxiety Normal?* ..................................................... 24

*What Medications Can a 15-Year-Old Take for Anxiety?* ........... 27

*What Are Signs of Anxiety in a Teenager?* ............................... 29

*How Can I Help My Teenager with Anxiety?* ........................... 32

*Consequences of Teen Anxiety* ................................................ 34

*Why Are Teens Prone to Anxiety?* ............................................ 36

**Chapter 3: How Society Contributes to Your Teen's Anxiety** ........................................................................................ 41

*What are the Main Causes of Teen Anxiety?* ........................... 42

*The Impact of Social Media on Teenage Anxiety* ..................... 49

*Impact of Anxiety on Teens* ..................................................... 49

*Long-term Effects of Anxiety on Teens* ................................... 54

*Causes of Shyness or Nervousness in Teens* ........................... 55

*Are You Born with Social Anxiety? Does It Ever Go Away?* ........ 56

**Chapter 4: How Parents Contribute to Teen Anxiety** .......... 59

*How Parents Can Give Teens Anxiety ................................ 61*

*Can Controlling Parents Cause Anxiety? ........................... 65*

*How Can Parents' Stress Hurt a Child? ............................. 67*

*What Are Signs of Bad Parenting? ..................................... 69*

*How a Parent Can Help a Teen with Anxiety ................... 71*

*Calming an Anxious Child .................................................. 73*

## Chapter 5: What to Do If My Teen Has Anxiety? ................. 75

*Common Signs of Anxiety .................................................... 76*

*Emotional Signs of Anxiety .................................................. 76*

*How to Treat Emotional Signs of Anxiety ......................... 78*

*Physical Warning Signs of Anxiety ..................................... 79*

*How to Treat Physical Signs of Anxiety ............................. 81*

*Behavioral Manifestations of Anxiety ................................ 82*

*How to Treat Behavioral Signs of Anxiety ........................ 84*

*Common Treatment Options for Anxiety ......................... 85*

## Chapter 6: Learn About and Teach Anxiety ......................... 93

*Talking to Your Teen about Anxiety ................................... 94*

*Delving Into the World of Anxiety ..................................... 97*

*Identifying Anxiety ............................................................... 98*

*What Not to Do ..................................................................... 99*

## Chapter 7: Strategies to Support an Anxious Teen ........... 111

*Set Realistic Expectations .................................................. 113*

*What Are You Avoiding? ................................................... 116*

## Chapter 8: Self-Soothing Techniques for Teens with Anxiety ....................................................................................... 127

*Practices for Long-term Effects ........................................ 128*

*Techniques for Immediate Relief ........................................................ 135*

**Chapter 9: Teenage Suicide ....................................................... 145**

*Teens at Risk................................................................................... 146*

*Signs of Depression......................................................................... 148*

*What to Look for in a Suicidal Teenager ........................................ 150*

*Diagnosis......................................................................................... 154*

*Treatment........................................................................................ 155*

*How Can I Help Prevent Teen Suicide?........................................... 156*

*When to Call a Doctor and How to Handle an Appointment ...... 159*

**Chapter 10: Parenting and Anxiety ........................................ 163**

*Self-Care Tips for Parents................................................................ 163*

**Conclusion................................................................................. 179**

**References ................................................................................ 183**

KATHERINE GUZMAN

# INTRODUCTION

Anxiety in teens and tweens is rapidly increasing with time. It is believed that one in five teenagers is highly likely to suffer from chronic anxiety once during their young age. Despite being well-informed and well-aware, some parents may still fail to decipher the real issue and help their kids cope.

Has your teen been complaining about consistent stomach aches or any other health issues? Are they constantly afraid of attending school or public places? Do you notice perpetual mood swings in your teen? Instead of rolling your eyes and thinking to yourself, "Here we go again," try to dig deeper as the issue may be more serious than you think. Start by comforting them by helping them to find solutions to solve the issues immediately. However, if they fail to budge or cooperate, you might get impatient, but that this will only make the situation worse for your teen. They are already feeling irked and frustrated, so you don't want to add to their existing discontentment.

If you wish to ease your child's agony, you must learn about the real issue and look for signs related to anxiety. Teens are already going through a lot in their adolescent years due to rising competition, peer pressure, and hormonal changes. It can worsen their anxiety and make the situation entirely threatening.

Since anxiety can harm your teen's physical, mental, and emotional health, it is necessary to recognize the signs early. Some may even show poor performance at school, affecting their chances of getting into a good university or excelling at their career as they grow up. Treating chronic anxiety is very important as it can abate the chances of suicidal ideas and self-harm.

This book is packed with all the information needed to recognize and delve deeper into the issue of anxiety and related disorders. Since this subject can be complicated and sensitive, pay attention to every aspect this book illustrates as it is bound to help every anxiety-related issue. Having been through similar problems related to teens, chronic anxiety, and related issues, this book provides practical insights since it is based on factual information and real-life experiences.

If you can relate to these factors, take your child's condition seriously without waiting to recognize further relevance. With time, failing to treat chronic anxiety can be life-threatening and cause irreversible damage. While teens struggle to control their feelings and lash out easily compared to adults, their treatment can be more effective as their fury is often related to a cry for help.

If you have been feeling similar angst and need to take the necessary steps to help your teen cope with the torment of anxiety, this book will teach you the right way to approach this issue. It has everything you need to know, from learning about the signs to seeking help in extreme situations. As parents, you will also learn some self-care tips and ways to treat your own issues to help your child overcome theirs. Read on to begin the journey toward healing your teen's anxiety.

# CHAPTER 1:

# UNDERSTANDING ANXIETY

The first step to cure any anxiety issue is understanding it in depth. At times, anxiety is disregarded as merely a mental "mood" that comes and goes. It is necessary for guardians and parents to understand anxiety's real meaning and dig deeper to decipher the crux of the issue. Since anxiety is often deep-rooted, it can be a bit difficult to treat. However, it's not impossible. To effectively treat this mental health issue means learning about what anxiety is and the causes that may have triggered it.

## What is Anxiety?

Anxiety is created by your body when it prepares you to face threats around you. In other words, your body tries to keep you safe in dangerous situations and motivates you to fight them. Let's say that you are walking on the road, tired after a long day at work and wanting to get into bed and rest. However, your lethargy and laziness instantly pass once you encounter any danger around you. For example, you spot a snake on the road, your body will instantly increase its energy levels and compel you to run, despite being tired. Even though random bursts of anxiety can be helpful, regularly facing this issue can affect your health and lifestyle in the long run. For example, new beginnings, such as moving or starting a new job, can make a person anxious. However, this anxious feeling can boost confidence and help a person perform better. Your body's reaction to something that is not an actual or obvious threat or challenge can trigger this mental health issue.

Anxiety is often confused with getting worried. Even though every individual is prone to feeling worried and nervous in certain situations, not everyone is necessarily an anxiety patient. In some cases, anxiety is often misunderstood by most people and treated like another temporary health issue. In reality, this mental health problem can degrade a person's quality of life and push them into a downward spiral if left untreated for a prolonged period. In extreme cases, anxiety can trigger serious health issues debilitating your life. As mentioned, it can be effectively treated once you learn more about the origins.

## What Causes Anxiety?

While normal or ordinary anxiety is a feeling commonly experienced by just about everyone, it can become a major issue if you keep feeling worried and fear the consequences all the time. Several aspects can result in anxiety, namely-

### 1. Genetics

Individuals with a family history of anxiety or other mental health issues are highly likely to experience anxiety. Even though they may have had a happy childhood, witnessing their parents undergoing anxiety can also have a major impact on their mental health.

## 2. Physical Health Conditions

People with certain physical health conditions, such as epilepsy, asthma, diabetes, and certain allergies, are more prone to developing anxiety. In turn, this can affect and worsen their physical health and make treatment difficult. However, being anxious and undergoing physical health issues can help your medical practitioner diagnose the issue easily.

## 3. Personality Traits

If you have inherited or developed certain personality traits growing up, you may develop anxiety. For example, being extremely shy or a perfectionist are some traits that may lead to anxiety disorders. However, not every individual with distinct traits is susceptible to developing anxiety.

## 4. Traumatic Experiences

If a person has undergone an extremely traumatic experience and finds it difficult to deal with past emotions, they may develop PTSD, which is a form of anxiety disorder. It can also occur due to stressful events that are too difficult to overcome. Some examples of such stressful events include emotional or physical abuse, pregnancy, personal or professional problems, or the demise of a loved one.

While these are the known reasons that trigger anxiety, several studies and research are ongoing to decipher the exact reason.

## Types of Anxiety Disorders

Anxiety disorders are emotional issues triggered by extreme worrying, feelings of fear, and staying anxious most of the time. While women are more prone to suffer from an anxiety disorder, men should also be mindful of this emotional issue.

Let's take a look at some common types of anxiety disorders that many teenagers and young adults face.

### 1. Panic Disorder

When your anxiety reaches a peak level, your body may respond by triggering symptoms like heavy breathing, fast heart rate, cold or hot flashes, nausea, and excessive sweating. These signs indicate that a person is experiencing a panic attack and should be treated by a mental health practitioner. Since panic attacks can occur anytime and anywhere, especially during intense situations, this disorder should be treated at the earliest. While some individuals experience just one panic attack in their lifetime, others may face recurring episodes that can worsen their situation and lifestyle.

## 2. Social Anxiety Disorder

This disorder is entrenched in the fear of being judged and not being "good enough" for others. It can lead to feelings of awkwardness and discomfort in social settings. Commonly known as social phobia, this disorder makes individuals avoid attending social events and keeps them isolated. The constant fear of doing something embarrassing and judgmental stares makes them shy or nervous. To alleviate such situations, they avoid going to new places and meeting people altogether. Occurrences like meeting an old friend at the grocery store and making small talk are also difficult for them.

## 3. Generalized Anxiety Disorder

This disorder is an emotional disorder where the person undergoes excessive worrying and feels burdened all the time. Individuals with generalized anxiety disorder often loathe themselves because they keep worrying about meager things, even about how they worry over such insignificant factors. Teenagers are more prone to this disorder due to the unwanted pressure they face daily. The inability to control the amount of worrying they do is also a sign of this disorder. Due to this, they are often unable to sleep or focus on their work.

## 4. Obsessive-Compulsive Disorder

Commonly known as OCD, this anxiety disorder puts the patient in a circuit of trundling certain actions. Their obsessive behavior can lead to anxious thoughts, which, in turn, increases panic. For example, placing certain items in an aligned way or feeling restless until certain things are organized are common signs and behavioral aspects of OCD. With time, this anxiety disorder results in the person performing repeated actions and developing irrational thoughts. Simple actions like going back and forth to check and double-check if they have locked the door or organizing their drawer in the order of specific colors are some examples of repeated behaviors in OCD.

## 5. Agoraphobia

Agoraphobia is the fear of experiencing a panic attack in a place where they might not receive any help. It keeps the person from attending social events or public places for long periods. They also prefer to keep away from crowds and long queues. This disorder can worsen if the person visits a place where they have experienced a panic attack before. Individuals who have Agoraphobia need someone to accompany them when waiting in queues or catching a bus. They may also feel more anxious when they cannot leave certain places at will.

While these five anxiety disorders are the most common, some may even experience other types such as separation anxiety disorder, post-traumatic stress disorder (PTSD), illness anxiety disorder, and certain phobias.

## Common Signs of Anxiety

### Feeling on Edge or Nervous Most of the Time

If you or your loved one feels nervous or worried regularly, consider it a sign of anxiety. At times, feeling nervous about the smallest or ludicrous things is a common sign in individuals with anxiety. Due to this, they fear going out in public spaces or meeting new people. You might have noticed that people with anxiety lack socializing skills because meeting new people and starting conversations makes them anxious. Their habit of obsessive thinking and impending panic can thereby affect their lifestyle quality.

## Facing Difficulty Concentrating

Your mind is constantly thinking about the downside and focusing on the negative aspects of the situation, diverting your attention and diminishing your concentration levels. Turning an incoming piece of information into a cohesive fact becomes even more difficult when you have anxiety, thereby affecting your ability to focus and complete even simple duties. This, in turn, results in delayed tasks and pushes your goals further away. Real-time reasoning is a sign of a healthy brain, but it can be affected by recurring thoughts related to fear and worry. In turn, your brain shifts focus to insignificant aspects.

## Feeling Overwhelmed

The inability to concentrate also adds to an overwhelming feeling, which can further worsen the condition. Irrespective of the task you are supposed to complete, the overwhelming feeling keeps you restrained and does not allow you to accomplish the simplest tasks. This feeling also veils the real trigger that provoked the negative emotion, which is why individuals often confuse it with anger. The stress hormone cortisol is released by your body when you feel worried and overwhelmed, as this can lead to extreme anxiety and worsen the situation. Equally, the hormone responsible for fighting anxiety is also reduced.

## Constantly Worrying About Things Going Bad

Even if the situation is in their favor, people who have anxiety find it difficult to look at the positive side. Instead, they focus on the negative aspects and worry about things going wrong even if there is no such possibility of it happening. In the long run, such individuals will face trouble sleeping, causing other issues like insomnia. With time, the person may turn into a pessimist and fail to acknowledge any situation's positive side affecting their personal and professional life.

## Heavy Breathing and Heart Palpitations

In some cases, individuals may show physical signs during anxiety attacks, such as heavy breathing, adrenaline rush, a boost in energy level, stomach twisting, and heart palpitations. Some people even face extreme sweating and shaking. As mentioned, these signs are related to the advent of panic attacks that can turn into recurring episodes if left untreated. Panic attacks are often confused with anxiety attacks as they share similar signs. If you or your loved ones experience an anxiety or panic attack, consult a medical practitioner as soon as you can.

Even though these are the most common signs and symptoms of anxiety, they can vary from person to person. Monitor the behavior and signs to diagnose their anxiety disorder. It will also help you get optimum treatment for the specific condition.

## Difference Between Anxiety and Fear

Most misinformed people confuse anxiety with fear, and these are used interchangeably. In reality, fear is a negative emotion triggered due to a known cause or situation. On the other hand, the real reason behind anxiety is often unknown or shrouded. Since both emotions lead to a stressful outcome, individuals get confused between anxiety and fear. The most common physiological signs and symptoms of both anxiety and fear are increased heart rate, sweating, muscle tension, and some may even experience shortness of breath.

While fear often leads to a negative occurrence due to the visibility of danger, anxiety is only limited to the possibility of experiencing something negative or dangerous. In other words, fear is related to an immediate threat, whereas anxiety is related to the prospects of finding yourself in a dangerous situation.

**Key Takeaway:** Anxiety is a common feeling that most people experience on a day-to-day basis. While it helps you overcome unwanted situations, recurring anxiety should be treated as it can ruin a person's health and lifestyle. Physical and emotional health issues, trauma, genetics, and environmental conditions are some common reasons for anxiety. It is imperative to learn about the various anxiety disorder types to diagnose and treat patients effectively. Furthermore, it's important to comprehend the common signs of anxiety to help yourself or your loved one.

# CHAPTER 2:

# TEENS AND ANXIETY

It's very common for teenagers to suffer from anxiety or anxiety disorders. Teenagers are more prone to develop anxiety because teenage years are the time to try new experiences, face new challenges, and take new opportunities. It's also the time when their brains start changing, and they seek more independence. Simple stages like secondary school, college, fitting in with other peers, and looking a certain way may be worrisome and stressful for a normal teenager. Additional to the responsibilities that fall on their shoulders at this age, they are pressured to become independent, like getting a job and living independently, making anxiety very common for teenagers. Especially since various adult emotions start developing during this period, this can cause anxiety to be common at this age. Although feelings of anxiousness do not last for most teenagers and tend to go away on their own, some teens struggle with persistent anxiety that becomes very intense, preventing them from participating in everyday activities. In this chapter, we discuss the struggles of teenagers with anxiety. What are the hidden anxiety signs? How can you interject and help your child with their difficult yet, completely normal mental condition?

## Is Teenage Anxiety Normal?

This question becomes more and more persistent since you're spending a lot of time at home with your teens during quarantine. Eventually, this leads you to start questioning behaviors that you may have never seen from your teens before. The lack of physical contact with friends makes it even harder for your teenager to navigate normal social dynamics. Even their bodies will experience several changes due to the lack of privacy and reduced physical activity, not to mention how overwhelming it might be for your son or daughter to meet your expectations where learning and teaching experience technical changes.

All these factors make it normal for most teenagers to suffer from anxiety.

## Anxiety Is Both Normal and Helpful

Anxiety is not only a normal physical response, but it is also helpful and puts your body into an alert state to prepare you for avoiding predator attacks. If you think about it, we all experience anxious emotions as we grow up. It's just that adults are more skilled in recognizing these emotions or physical signs. Nowadays, anxiety is much needed for many modern occasions that require you to perform at your best. For example, those butterflies you feel in your stomach before a presentation alert you to be adequately prepared. Normally, most of us experience anxiety before important events, but it's also normal for teenagers to experience slightly higher levels of anxious feelings, especially in situations where they feel like their future plans are not certain.

## When Does Teenage Anxiety Become Intrusive?

Anxiety is a cause of concern when it starts limiting your teenager's function and affecting many areas of their life. Your teen may have an anxiety disorder if they tend to show exaggerated reactions to simple threats and complications. For example, starting college or high school may be a difficult and nerve-racking experience for many young adults. However, a teenager with an anxiety disorder may even cease to function due to stress. They may emotionally and verbally shut down during classes. Some kids with severe anxiety may even attempt to avoid school. This is what health professionals would call an Anxiety Disorder. They use this term to refer to several conditions, including agoraphobia, separation anxiety disorder, social anxiety, panic disorder, selective mutism, and generalized anxiety disorder. At this point, these conditions may cause many parents to worry. However, it's important to stay reminded that anxiety is common among teenagers and can be treated easily.

## The Difference Between Normal Anxiety and an Anxiety Disorder

It would be ideal for parents to be able to tell the difference between acceptable anxiety levels and intrusive ones so that they know when they should contact a mental health professional. As a parent, it is your priority to adjust to your child's behavior and accommodate their anxiety. You can tell if your teenager has an anxiety disorder by checking if they're quitting or avoiding daily routines or constantly complaining about unexplained fatigue, headaches, or stomachaches. A teenager with an anxiety disorder will also have impacted sleeping habits, school attendance, personal hygiene, or a drop in their school grades. Typically, you'll notice your teen becoming more sensitive or emotional or even defensive more often.

# What Medications Can a 15-Year-Old Take for Anxiety?

## 1. Serotonin-Norepinephrine Reuptake Inhibitors or SNRIs

SNRIs contain a chemical substance that increases serotonin and norepinephrine and prevents the brain from reabsorbing them again at the same time. They can take up to a few weeks to show their full effects and may lead to similar side effects to another category of anxiety medications called Selective Serotonin Reuptake Inhibitors (SSRIs). Your child's doctor will check for potential side effects from both medications before choosing between SNRIs and SSRIs. The doctor will also consider things like your family history regarding how these medications have been received and the potential interactional effect with any other medications your teen takes.

## 2. Selective Serotonin Reuptake Inhibitors or SSRIs

SSRIs were initially antidepressants that improved mood by inhibiting the reuptake of the serotonin transmitter. They are the most com-mon type and usually the first type of medication prescribed to teenagers who have anxiety disorders. Their side effects, similar to SNRIs, include headaches, nausea, and sleeping problems. These side effects can take weeks to ease up, but it's important to ensure your teen does not quit their medication without consulting the doctor because sudden or premature discontinuation of many medications, especially antidepressants, can lead to uncomfortable withdrawal symptoms or flu-like symptoms.

## 3. Tricyclic Antidepressants or TCAs

Tricyclic antidepressants are usually prescribed when SNRIs and SSRIs are unhelpful. Your child's doctor may recommend an FDA-approved medication called clomipramine. Clomipramine soothes obsessive-compulsive disorder and social anxiety. However, TCAs pose a risk of serious side effects, such as sedation, constipation, and cardiac abnormalities. Therefore, patients who are prescribed TCAs are usually provided with regular EKGs to monitor their cardiac health. Your child's doctor must inform you about all the potential side effects and whether switching to TCAs is the best available option or not.

**4. Benzodiazepines**

It's not common for mental health doctors to prescribe benzodiazepines as a first treatment for a teenager with anxiety. These drugs can cause patients to develop a tolerance and become addicted to their medication. So, what are benzodiazepines? They are common sedating and anxiety medications that you've probably heard of before. These include Diazepam or Valium, alprazolam or Xanax, lorazepam or Ativan, and clonazepam or Klonopin. Incorrect discontinuation of any of these drugs can lead your teen to develop serious withdrawal symptoms. Most of the time, these drugs are prescribed along with SSRIs or SNRIs until the inhibitors reach their full effect.

# What Are Signs of Anxiety in a Teenager?

The most obvious emotional signs of anxiety include irritability, restlessness, feeling on edge, difficulty concentrating, panic attacks, and unexplained outbursts. Here are other signs you may notice in a teenager with an anxiety disorder.

## Physical Signs

Most of the anxiety's physical complaints can mimic the physical complaints of any average teen. However, the signs keep increasing as the person grows if they assuredly have an anxiety disorder. For example, headaches. While this might sound like a regular health complaint, frequent headaches are a cause of concern and may indicate that your teen has anxiety. Other common physical complaints include constant fatigue, gastrointestinal problems, not feeling well for no obvious medical cause, unexplained aches, and changing eating habits. Pay attention to any of these signs and follow up with a mental health professional if you notice any repetitive patterns.

## Social Changes

Anxiety can be detected much easier by monitoring your teen's social interactions and activities because an anxiety disorder can significantly affect your child's relationships with their friends. A vital sign is if your teen was once a social person but gradually lost interest in their favorite activities or declined plans with their friends. It should also be obvious if they keep avoiding extracurricular activities and social interactions with their usual friends. Other signs include isolation from peer groups and spending a lot of time on their own.

## Bad Performance at School

Anxiety can have a serious impact on your teen's performance at school. A teenager with an anxiety disorder would typically have disturbed sleeping patterns and eating habits, in addition to constantly missing school due to various physical issues they face dealing with everyday anxiety. It is very predictable for teenagers with untreated anxiety disorders to have poor academic performance. School workload can become very overwhelming for your teen with all their missed days and school avoidance thanks to their anxiety-related illness and persistent worry. It may help you as a parent to look for signs like frequently missed assignments, complaints about overwhelming workload, negative jumps in grades, procrastination, and difficulty concentrating.

# How Can I Help My Teenager with Anxiety?

A teenager who has an anxiety disorder may not be able to feel better on their own. This is why it's your duty as a parent to accommodate their anxiety and help them feel more comfortable at home. However, most parents are not educated enough to deal with constant stress, nervousness, and tension. Here is how you can be there for your teenager as they struggle with their daily anxiety symptoms.

## Help Them Relax More

Achieving relaxation is not as simple as most people think. For example, you're not helping your teen relax by letting them chill in front of the TV or their computer screen. This can be even more stressful for them, depending on what they are watching. Tobacco, alcohol, and drugs may have the same impact on a person with anxiety - they provide a false, temporary state of relaxation. Naturally, what their bodies need is daily relaxation or breathing techniques that have a physical effect on their brain, and this can be achieved by practicing yoga, meditation, or even tai chi.

## Make Sure They Are Connecting with Others

Hanging out or participating in organized activities with friends and family can be very effective in deepening your teenager's bonds with the people they feel the closest to. It will eventually make them feel more secure and supported, which can ease their symptoms. Plus, the fun and sharing in the whole experience of connecting with others will elevate their mood and increase their serotonin levels. Talking with someone who cares and listens to them will help them cope with their stress and feel more understood. If you happen to be that person, take the opportunity to assure them that we all have these feelings and that it's normal to have anxious thoughts or emotions.

## Help Them Get Enough Sleep and Exercise

Your child's overall health plays a great role in how much peace of mind they're getting. If they don't feel peaceful enough, their body and mind won't handle their mental state's ups and downs. It's extremely important to keep reminding them to get enough sleep at night. They should be sleeping from 7 to 8 hours every night. Sleeping for longer or shorter periods could cause headaches and even ruin their mood. They should eat vegetables, whole grains, fruit, and lean protein to provide their bodies with long-term energy rather than the short bursts they get from eating too much sugar or drinking caffeine. If possible, exercise-ing will help them relieve stress and cope with their anxious feelings.

### Help Them Spend More Time Out in Nature

Nothing can help you feel more peaceful and grounded than a quiet walk in the park, or maybe a hike in the woods, because nature is simply the quickest medicine for anxiety and feeling overwhelmed. It would be very helpful to encourage your teen to get outside, choose somewhere they find safe and relaxing, and engage more with nature. Your teen can use this opportunity to exercise, try trail biking, or even snowshoeing to release some of their energy and decrease stress and tension.

## Consequences of Teen Anxiety

### Panic Attacks

Panic attacks happen due to another disorder called Panic Disorder. Many teenagers have another anxiety disorder along with their panic disorder, which causes patients to experience panic attacks, constant feelings of anxiety, and terror. They may also experience physical symptoms, such as chest pain, heart palpitations, and shortness of breath. Panic attacks can strike an anxious patient at any time, so a coping technique is crucial to ending these episodes whenever they occur.

## Central Nervous System Damage

If a person suffers from anxiety and panic attacks for a long period, their brains regularly release stress hormones. This reaction causes anxiety and panic symptoms, such as dizziness, headaches, and depression, to become more frequent. When your teen feels stressed or anxious, their brain produces significant amounts of chemicals and hormones designed to prepare the body for threats. Although stress hormones can help them handle stressful situations and events, long-term exposure to these chemicals can be harmful to their bodies and contribute to weight gain.

## Excretory and Digestive System Problems

Did you know that anxiety also impacts your child's digestive and excretory system? If your teen has an anxiety disorder, they may experience nausea, stomachaches, diarrhea, and many other digestion-related issues. They may even lose their appetite and start shedding weight rapidly. Some studies show a relation between anxiety and irritable bowel syndrome or IBS, causing your teen to suffer from constipation, diarrhea, and vomiting. In some cases, anxiety can lead to serious gastric issues that cause abdominal discomfort and vomiting.

**Immune System Deficiency**

When you face a threatening or stressful situation, your anxiety triggers a fight-or-flight process that increases your breathing and pulse rate to get more oxygen to your brain. Your brain does that by flooding hormones and chemicals into your system. Although these chemicals can boost your immune system temporarily, they can weaken it in the long run and cause you to become vulnerable to viral infections and illnesses. If you constantly feel stressed or experience anxiety for a long time, your body never returns to normal functioning, even if the stress passes. This is what anxiety can do to your teenager if you leave it untreated for too long.

## Why Are Teens Prone to Anxiety?

As a multitasking parent or adult, you might wonder why teens have to be anxious all the time or what can stress them that much. They don't have to worry about paying rent, putting food on the table, raising children, or any adult responsibilities. So, what causes them to be so vulnerable to anxiety and panic disorders? Maybe, if you knew the reason, you could offer help and ease your son's or daughter's struggles. Therefore, it's important to acknowledge the factors in their life that make this stage difficult and stressful for them. Here are some of these factors.

## Brain Development and Hormones

A teenager's brain is not fully developed until they reach their mid-twenties, making it hard for your teen to take on adult responsibilities. Suddenly, they're required to look after themselves when they don't have the brain development or skills necessary to care for themselves fully. Teenagers and younger adults face many moments when they don't know what they are doing. Add to that the tremendous frustration and lack of ability that come along with adulting. It significantly increases your teenager's anxiety levels and causes their hormonal levels to fluctuate, leading them to experience depression, anger, or even anxiety for no reason.

## High Expectations and Parental Disapproval

Teenagers go through an endless cycle of stress due to the amount of pressure they put on themselves by building high expectations or trying to match society's expectations of them. They want to do great in school, go to a prestigious university, and participate in all the social events around them. They get part-time jobs, volunteer in community events, finish their chores at home and manage to maintain active social lives. Such expectations can stress your teenager and leave them with no time to sleep or even have a quiet time on their own. They also experience one of the most awkward stages of their lives where they want to meet their parents' expectations and rebel against their authority simultaneously.

Anxiety is very normal at this stage of your teen's life. Keep reminding yourself of this. Teenagers go through one of the toughest periods of their life. They meet new stressful situations and face new challenges impacting their bodies in all sorts of ways. They also have to keep up with your expectations and fit in with their peers to avoid peer pressure. It can drop a heavy burden on your 14 or 15-year-old's shoulders and cause them to develop an anxiety disorder. This is when your role as a parent must accommodate their needs and become their source of comfort. Understand this age carefully and find trusted resources to learn about anxiety disorders that specifically relate to teenagers. It will help you interfere in their routines healthily without causing them any additional stress.

# CHAPTER 3:

# HOW SOCIETY CONTRIBUTES TO YOUR TEEN'S ANXIETY

Society plays a major role in elevating every teen's anxiety and placing unwanted pressure that impacts their short and long-term health. Since puberty is a difficult period to deal with, teens are on the brink of developing anxiety, depression, or other mental health issues.

Questions related to the causes of teenage anxiety, signs, short and long-term effects, and the correlation between shyness and anxiety arise among parents. This chapter will address some important and thought-provoking instances related to society's contribution to teens' anxiety. Since most teens fail to understand or convey their thoughts and feelings, it is time to debunk some myths related to society's impact on teens.

## What are the Main Causes of Teen Anxiety?

While several aspects can trigger the effects of stress and anxiety among teens and young adults, it all boils down to the societal impact and its whimsical brunt. Let's take a look at some common causes propelled by the menacing face of our communities.

### 1. Societal and Peer Pressure

Unwanted peer pressure and the need to be perfect stems from society's grotesque expectations. Extreme emphasis on looking pretty, tall, and perfect can affect a teen's mental health and shake their confidence. They are already undergoing several physical changes, such as a shift in vocal range, height, recurring acne, body odor, sexual urges, etc. It becomes too much to handle, especially since it is new for adolescents. Even though there is no "said" societal pressure, teens get the urge to feel pressured through the fear of judgment and comparison with their friends. This comparison can lead to teens taking drastic steps, too.

Furthermore, the increasing rate of violence, bullying and open threats can also take a toll on the young and developing minds. Traumatic incidents like school shootings, attacks, protests, etc., are alarming and can easily intimidate children and teens. The world we live in is a scary place, and the menace, directly and indirectly, influences young minds. At the same time, society and parents fail to provide coping strategies to help teens face and overcome such challenging situations. Growing up in such a volatile environment will undeniably add to any child's or teen's anxiety.

## 2. Disapproval from Parents and the Elderly

Teens and young adults are always on their parents' radar as they expect them to succeed and get good grades. The need to get into a good university, establish a successful career, look presentable, etc., are common forms of expectations that most parents have of their teens. However, every person is different, and while some may achieve good grades even without studying, others may fail despite working hard. Parents must examine this threshold and ponder over the legitimate issue instead of putting more stress on the young minds. Like adults, teens have become extremely busy and are expected to participate in sports, volunteer, complete house chores, and study at the same time.

Most parents feel competitive and push their children to perform better. At times, these expectations cross the line and thrust their kids into a mental dilemma. While excelling at school and university is a milestone most teens and parents set, the inability to do so may push the adolescents into a downward spiral. If they keep failing and cannot cope with the stress, they may receive disappointing grunts and disapproval from their parents. Even if the teen wishes to follow a consistent pace, the outlook they receive can steadily turn into anxiety, and this leads to sleep deprivation, which can worsen the situation.

### 3. Hormonal Changes

Since teens undergo many hormonal changes during the adolescent phase, they may also experience changes in their mental health. Issues, such as depression, stress, anxiety, etc., advance and ebb throughout this delicate phase and invade any teen's lifestyle. Teens are often seen as irritated and angry, especially with their parents. Hormonal fluctuations, testosterone and estrogen surges, menstrual shifts, etc., are some phenomena that are already too difficult to deal with. Since this development phase is new for teens, they cannot decipher the right way to handle it, and it results in passive-aggressiveness and arguments with their loved ones.

Moreover, most teens are immature and unable to confront their feelings, and when paired with mental health fluctuations, the situation can worsen and create anxiety. The responses and reactions are majorly heightened and are upheaved with external stimulants like unsupportive parents and societal peer pressure. All these factors combined can elevate stress hormone receptors, affecting their mental health. Simultaneously, hormones responsible for relaxation and happiness start depleting, adding to the existing discord. It is believed that hormonal changes are one of the major reasons for teenage anxiety and increasing stress.

## 4. Vices

The stigma that most teens are exposed to during this phase is the use of alcohol, cigarettes, and drugs. Even though they know that their parents will not support this behavior and disapprove of such acts, they still take up drinking and drug usage. While some do drugs and drink alcohol under their friends' influence, others simply wish to experiment. In the latter scenario, it can turn into a long-lasting habit that becomes difficult to overcome.

Teens are easily influenced by the people who are part of their lives. If they hang out with friends who are a bad influence, they are highly likely to pick up similar vices and bad habits. Let's talk about their definition of being "cool." Being cool is shrouded by teen angst. They wish to look and feel grown up physically and mentally. Teens believe that this will earn them respect and help them gain the attention of the opposite gender. They define their curiosity and eagerness to mature fast as being cool. Since adults often drink and smoke, teens get caught up in the same spiral. The situation can be even more threatening if the teens see their parents regularly drinking and smoking. In extreme cases, this can turn into a major addiction and ruin an individual's life. When deprived of cigarettes or alcohol, an addicted person will experience severe anxiety.

## 5. Immaturity and Brain Development

It is known that a person's brain fully develops once they cross their twenties, and the reason most teens are immature and unable to take care of themselves and others around them. They talk back, are disrespectful, cannot distinguish right from wrong, and are usually frustrated. Since managing and completing certain tasks on their own is difficult, their agitation can steadily turn into anxiety. At times, this can also keep them apart from their loved ones.

Parents often complain about feeling distant from their teens since they prefer to hang out with their friends and stay out until late at night. The feeling of being secluded and grown apart can be too difficult for parents to accept, especially if their child has been extremely close to them in the past. At times, it can reflect in the parents' behavior, which increases their child's anxiety. Teens need their space, and when deprived of it, they will feel anxious.

Paired with the physical and body changes that most teens go through, it can take a major toll on their mental health. Their immaturity also leads them to talk back and disrespect adults. Teens with strict parents may often get punished for their crude behavior, which worsens the situation.

## 6. Depression

Teenage depression is quite common and is steadily turning into a scenario that affects their adult years as well. The link between societal pressure and depression or anxiety is profoundly intertwined. While some believe that the long-lasting effects of anxiety can lead to depression, others claim that the opposite is also true. Due to this, the symptoms of both issues often overlap, making the diagnosis process even more challenging. Parents often cannot decipher the real issue and fail to understand what their child is going through during their adolescent phase. In any case, anxiety and depression in teens are deep-rooted and should be taken extremely seriously.

Some common symptoms related to depression are constant frustration, irritability, fatigue, feeling hopeless or sad, being alone or isolated, sleeping too much or too little, low concentration levels, headaches, and even suicidal thoughts.

## The Impact of Social Media on Teenage Anxiety

Another major reason for teens to feel anxious is the virtual pressure created by social media. The virtual appreciation and validation they receive on social media turn into short-term gratification where most teens find pleasure in.

In extreme cases, social media can ruin a teen's self-esteem as everything seems perfect in the virtual world. They fail to differentiate between reality and virtual representation. In other words, their general sense of worldview can drastically change, leading to constant comparison and unhappiness.

Like the teens of today coin the abbreviation "FOMO," the Fear of Missing Out on the latest updates or trends and not being online is detrimental to their mental health, and this is also why we see teens spending more time on social media instead of studying.

## Impact of Anxiety on Teens

### Poor Sleeping Habits

This is a common sign among most teens who suffer from anxiety. Recurring thoughts and constant fidgeting keep them awake at night and filling their brains with unwanted thoughts. This behavior also stems from overthinking and digging into the past. They may keep recalling embarrassing moments or argue with themselves about how they could have debated winning an argument more effectively. Even though these are common signs with both teens and adults, obsessive thinking is dangerous and affects their sleeping patterns. In extreme cases, teens with anxiety will develop insomnia affecting their short and long-term health and increases stress.

**Poor Eating Habits**

Not all teens care about their food habits. They may binge on sugar and hog on chips when they feel bored or unhappy, redirecting their anxious thoughts towards eating, which affects their health in the long run. For instance, while some may have anorexia and lose a lot of weight within a short period, others gain weight due to binge eating. The sudden fluctuations in body weight are extremely unhealthy and worsen their anxiety due to an improper body image. Let's not forget that most teens are anxious about their body weight and beauty issues. Teens with chronic anxiety may also consistently complain about stomach aches, headaches, and other health issues, that emerge from poor eating and sleeping habits.

## Low Grades and Performance in School

Some may even feel overwhelmed by the pressure of completing their tasks on time leading to poor grades and low performance in school and university. The inability to perform better in school also stems from extra peer pressure and unreasonably high expectations from parents. Even if the child is trying hard, they may not get the anticipated scores, which aggravates their anxiety. They will also be compared to the teens who perform well and get the best grades adding to their anxiety. Along with getting poor scores, they may also show indiscipline, such as skipping school or tardiness.

## Getting into Trouble

Teens often get in trouble and unnecessary fights over petty issues. However, if it turns into a consistent pattern, it can result from some deeper dispute. In essence, this disruptive behavior is a coping mechanism that is displayed to a varying degree. While some may cope with their anxiety by showcasing poor sleeping or eating habits, others display disruptive behavior and get in trouble from time to time. You will constantly receive complaints related to unnecessary tiffs and even punching or throwing things from your teen's school. At home, they are likely to throw tantrums and talk back. In such cases, it is difficult for the parent to control their child, which is why learning about the signs of anxiety and treating it from the initial stages is more helpful.

## Boredom or Feeling Unexcited

Being bored and not feeling excited about anything is another byproduct of anxiety. The feeling of not doing anything and lying in bed with recurring thoughts is something most teens are guilty of. Irritability, frustration, and agitation are common side effects of feeling bored. Since they prefer to be alone and hardly step out the boredom increases. In essence, boredom and anxiety are cohesive, and one can lead to the other. It is believed that agitated restlessness, anxiety, and boredom are interconnected. Even though the tedium-inducing effects are not well-defined by researchers to date, they can definitely make an impact on every teen's imagination power, creativity, concentration levels, and productivity.

The correlation of boredom with anxiety can be distinctively laid out in two different viewpoints. In the first case, boredom can make a person extremely lazy and lethargic, to the point that they cannot keep their eyes open, resulting in prolonged hours of sleep. On the contrary, being bored can result in restlessness and constant fidgeting. The second case is highly relevant to chronic anxiety and is expressed through signs like tapping your feet, pacing in the hallway, or feeling confused. Even though you try to concentrate and attempt to finish a task, the surging thoughts may stop you. With the drawback and lack of concentration, some people may even develop relevant mental issues, such as attention-deficit hyperactivity disorder (ADHD).

## Social Isolation

As mentioned earlier, social isolation may also emerge from anxiety and result in social anxiety disorder. Teens who fear not being likable or constantly judged are more prone to developing this form of anxiety disorder. Simple things like receiving glances when eating or shaking hands when meeting new people can make them super anxious. It will shake their confidence and deteriorate their communication skills. The feeling of being rejected when making small mistakes can eat them up from inside. It is more dreadful than we think it is. Dodging fear is a natural phenomenon that most humans proactively seek. However, considering actual people as a threat when they mean no harm to you makes the matter serious. Unable to cope with this challenge, most teens get into a "fight or flight" mode that can result in social isolation and loneliness.

## Long-term Effects of Anxiety on Teens

### Substance Use and Addiction

While trying to drink and smoke once or twice is a common phenomenon among most teens, prolonged use leads to addiction, which can ruin their lives.

### Depression

As mentioned, when left untreated for a prolonged period, anxiety can steadily turn into depression and push the teen into misery. At times, depression can linger for many years and also ruin their adult life.

### Suicidal Thoughts

With anxiety and depression, some teens may compile all the thoughts together, leading to suicidal intentions. The fear of being judged, the inability to perform better at school, failing to meet their parents' expectations, societal pressure, etc., can pile up and impose an overwhelming feeling. Those without parental support or lack of motivation may find it easier to leave the world than deal with their day-to-day qualms. It may seem ridiculous, but some teens are also anxious about the thought of the world ending. With the rising pandemic crisis, violence, climate change, and other major issues surrounding young children and teens' delicate minds, some take it acutely.

## Causes of Shyness or Nervousness in Teens

Even though being shy or nervous isn't necessarily a bad sign, it can affect a teen's personality and hinder their communication skills at a social level. The main cause of shyness, timidness, or nervousness is low self-confidence or self-esteem. Shyness is yet another form of coping mechanism that shouldn't be encouraged in teens. While genetics and the environment they grow up in are the main factors resulting in teens being shy, the people they hang out with and peer pressure also play a major role. More importantly, low self-esteem can result in passive behavior that keeps teens from speaking up, even if they know they are not being treated right. In the long run, it can also affect their personal and professional life. Teens with passive behavior believe that their opinions don't matter and lack decision-making skills, and this can result from a poor upbringing or inspired by the negative qualities of their parents.

## Are You Born with Social Anxiety? Does It Ever Go Away?

No one is born with social anxiety. In essence, inheriting relevant genetic traits can make the problem more intense. Stress, nervousness, and social phobia arise due to other factors as a person grows up but is elevated with the inherited genetics making it difficult to treat. When treated correctly, social anxiety does pass with time. Some people confuse social anxiety with awkwardness. While the former is steadily built due to several factors, the latter is a personality trait that can be difficult to overcome. By building confidence in teens and motivating them, they can surpass this social anxiety phase and elevate their communication skills.

**Key Takeaway:** The hideous truth of society's negative impact on teen anxiety is amiably cloaked by words like apprehension and expectations. As you can see, one anxiety-related issue is connected to other mental health problems. Failing to curb anxiety and the signs that follow can majorly disrupt your teen's mental health and quality of life. Since every teen portrays different signs of anxiety and copes with it using varying strategies, deciphering and handling the issue can be more challenging for the parent. While some teens may throw tantrums, others may completely isolate themselves. Social media adds to the existing issue and makes the situation formidable.

# CHAPTER 4:

# HOW PARENTS CONTRIBUTE TO TEEN ANXIETY

It is a long-established fact that the environment in which we live directly affects our mental health. Since parents take up a huge part of their teen's life, naturally, they can significantly affect their teen's anxiety. Even if your child spends most of their time in their bedroom or outside of the house, you are automatically associated with their idea of what a home should be. A home is supposed to be a comfort zone and a safe haven, but unfortunately, for teens that struggle with anxiety, a home can often be perceived as a trigger. The extent to which you are involved or uninvolved in your teen's life can feed into their anxiety. Words, actions, and behavior that may seem innocent and habitual can stimulate their anxiety, too. Living with an anxious teen is not easy and can sometimes be frustrating. However, once you truly understand how their minds work, acknowledge their fears, and explore your actions, you will realize that their train of thought is a justifiable response.

Living with anxiety can be a nightmare for the most part. With the growing number of teens diagnosed with anxiety disorders, it can be very easy for some parents to believe that their child's mental illness is their fault. When approaching your teen's anxiety, it's important to remember that you are not to blame for their disorder. Though, you should also keep in mind that some of your parenting habits may add to the problem. As a parent of an anxious teen, accept that you can either continue being part of the problem or step up to become part of the solution. Taking accountability and admitting that some of your actions may not be in your child's best interest is not easy. However, it is the first step toward relieving some of the pressure off your teen. This chapter will explore how you may be unintentionally hurting your teen and how you can help them.

## How Parents Can Give Teens Anxiety

### Too Caring

When it comes to your child's anxiety and emotions, it is important to remember that not everyone is the same. If one thing triggers a teen's anxiety, it does not necessarily mean that it negatively affects your child. Your best bet is to explore the different possibilities and closely recall how your child reacts in certain situations. Surprisingly, some teens get anxious when their parents care too much. Showing empathy when your child experiences a hurtful or heartbreaking situation is only normal. However, for some children, too much empathy is distressing. If you have noticed that your teen has suddenly stopped sharing things with you, especially their troubles, it's probably because of how you reacted to these situations in the past. It doesn't mean that you must stop showing that you care. It just means that you should show fewer signs of worry and anguish. If your teen decides to share their worries with you only to find that you're also worried, it will make things worse for them. The best thing to do is remain strong for them instead of falsely communicating to them that anxiety is the only way to face the issue. Besides, keeping their worries to themselves will further set off their anxiety.

**Extreme Advocating**

Another way you may be accidentally giving your teen anxiety is by taking it to the extreme when advocating for them. Every child finds comfort in the fact that their parents stand up for them no matter what. Similarly, standing up for your child is a parental instinct. However, don't forget that teens value their space, freedom, and independence now more than ever. Your eagerness to stand up for them when they didn't ask you to or explicitly asked you not to can raise their anxiety levels. Your persistence to advocate for them can break their self-confidence and show them that you don't believe they can resolve their issues on their own, leading them to avoid confiding in you. Your first instinct shouldn't be rushing to advocate on their behalf but rather to help them find a solution. Let them know that you believe they'll eventually resolve it on their own.

## Focusing On Weaknesses

Every parent wants to help their child tackle their weaknesses. While this type of support may be needed at times, it can easily become overbearing. Your teen doesn't want you to sign them up for private tutoring after getting one bad grade or buying them a motivational book when they feel down. Although this may be done with good intentions, your teen will automatically focus on the negative aspects. To boost their confidence and ease their anxiety, encourage them to play on their strengths instead of focusing on their weaknesses. One bad grade doesn't mean that they're weak at a certain subject. Even if they were, let them know that they don't have to be great at everything. Teach them to be content enough with what they are good at, reminding them that everyone has their own strengths and weaknesses. If your child likes to paint, offer to enroll them in professional painting classes. Enhancing their skills is better than trying to work on their weaknesses. It will give them a great confidence boost, which may even carry over to their weak points.

## Overemphasizing Strengths

We mentioned above that you should focus on your teens' strengths and encourage them to enhance them. However, be aware that there's a very thin line between encouragement and expectations. When you over-encourage or overly show off your child, they may feel like you are setting very high expectations for them, and this will provoke their anxiety and may even lead them to lose interest in this specific skill. Telling your friends that your teen is going to become a world-famous artist or gymnast is pressuring. Compliment them when they excel, though, don't make them feel like you are expecting more.

## Fear of Disappointment

All parents work very hard to ensure their children have great values and morals. Encouraging good values is extremely important and is something that any parent must do. Be that as it may, you must know where to draw the line. Stressing over certain values can result in your child obsessing over them. They may associate these values with their identity. On top of that, if they mess up, they will feel they have let you and themself down. Teens are susceptible to making poor choices. However, they should never feel too anxious to talk to you about them.

## Can Controlling Parents Cause Anxiety?

A teenager's autonomy and sense of control may be their ultimate desire. To most teens, control and freedom may be among the things they value the most in life. The majority of anxious teens feel the need to control their surroundings to feel at peace. Feeling out of control can cause anxiety to eat away at them, and controlling parents may be one of the causes. There are many ways to express love, and to some parents, being overly controlling is one way. Controlling parents don't necessarily exert control over their children to make their lives miserable. They do it because they think they know what's best for them. However, this excessive control can severely damage their child's mental, emotional, and social health.

Control comes in many forms. It can be behavioral or psychological and internal or external. Behavioral control is when a parent is determined to monitor their teen's social life, whereabouts, and behavior. When you exert this type of control over your teen, you are unnecessarily creating trust issues. Your child will constantly feel that you don't trust them and will always feel afraid that they may be doing something wrong- even when they're not. This type of control leaves them living in a constant state of anxiety. Psychological control is when a parent invades their teen's emotional and psychological state or development. Many parents with teens with mental disorders often validate their child's psychological issues. For instance, the majority of depressed teens are surrounded by family members who believe they are melodramatic or ungrateful. Similarly, children with anxiety have to suffer in silence because their parents tell them that their worries are silly. This type of control manipulates a child's psychological experience and causes them to believe that their feelings and mental health are not valid, further worsening their anxiety. You don't have to express verbal or external control to trigger your child. Internal control, such as expressing feelings of shame or guilt, is enough to hurt them.

There are many things that parents do daily without realizing that it's an eminent form of control. If you expect your child to obey you blindly and don't allow your teen to question or participate in decisions that affect them, then you are a controlling parent. Not allowing them to make their own decisions, discouraging them from becoming independent, and helping them without their permission can also severely break their confidence. If you prevent them from participating in certain activities because you "said so," it may cause them to act out. Using manipulations, such as love withdrawals and guilt-tripping, using punishments as a form of discipline, and constantly criticizing them will likely cause them to exhibit anti-social behavior and high anxiety tendencies.

## How Can Parents' Stress Hurt a Child?

Many comprehensive research and studies suggest that a parent's behavior can greatly affect a child's mental health. Mental illnesses are not developed overnight, but they are an accumulation of several thoughts, feelings, and observations over the years. Like most things, behavior and responses are taught. For example, if anger is your response to a specific situation, your child will be conditioned that this is how they should act when they find themselves in a similar circumstance. A stressed parent can affect an anxious child in a stage that's as early as pregnancy. A stressed pregnant woman can give birth to a child with several behavioral and psychological problems, including anxiety, ADHD, mood disorders, and risk for autism spectrum disorder. Stressed parents during the first few years of a child's life affect the child's genes. The signs resulting from such alterations, such as negative impacts on brain development and insulin production, can show throughout their later years and adolescence.

When you are stressed, you're likely to trigger a fight or flight response, which is the same response that is activated when someone is feeling anxious. Tension and anxiety are very closely related, so your teen will also certainly be on edge when you are constantly stressed. Parents who fight a lot, creating a stressful and tense atmosphere, are more likely to have children who show signs of depression and anxiety. A role of a parent in their teen's life is, directly and indirectly, incredibly significant.

The best thing you can do for your child, no matter how old they are or the developmental stage they're in, is to provide them with a sense of calmness, safety, and the lack of stress. Some studies show that perhaps this is even more important than providing them with unconditional love and emotions. This sense of tranquility allows their brains to develop and function in a familiar environment, resulting in a normally wired brain. Brains that develop in a constant state of stress are wired to always be prepared for an ambiguous sense of crippling danger, causing your child to be constantly anxious.

## What Are Signs of Bad Parenting?

In most cases, parents, and their parenting habits, are a great contributory factor to teens' anxiety. Adopting bad parenting habits doesn't automatically make you a bad parent. Bad parents are parents who realize that their actions are negatively impacting their child yet choose to do nothing about it. Being a parent is a 24/7 job that doesn't come with a handbook or clear guidelines, so it's normal to feel like parenting efforts are below par. The problem with being a parent is that every choice matters, and every mistake can result in long-term effects. If you feel like you may be doing something wrong, the following are bad parenting signs to watch out for.

### Being Over or Under Involved

Determining how involved you should be in your teen's life is very tricky. You don't want to be in the dark, not knowing anything about your child, and risk having them get themselves in severe trouble. On the other hand, you don't want to be involved to the extent where they feel suffocated. As long as you don't neglect your child's basic needs or take complete control of their decisions, trust that you will find the right balance. Establish trust and boundaries, and navigate until you find something that works for you and your child. Aim to become your child's friend and get involved because they want you to be one of the best things to happen to them.

## Little or Rigid Discipline

Like involvement in your child's life, you need to find the right balance for discipline. Undisciplined children don't understand boundaries, which creates many problems for them as they grow up. Undisciplined adolescents can often get themselves into great trouble. Children who lack discipline typically look after themselves at a very young age. Meanwhile, parents who overly discipline their children or enforce rigid and strict discipline prevent their children from creating their own journeys and experiences, resulting in either an extremely rebellious child or a very anxious one. Therefore, teach your child about what's wrong and right, and explain the consequences and the rewards. The best you can do is be there for your child and be someone who they can talk to about their fears, failures, adventures, and mistakes.

**Attention and Affection Withdrawal**

One fatal mistake that many parents make is associating their child's mistakes with expressing their feelings towards them. Ignoring your child and withdrawing feelings of affection from them when they do something wrong only shows them that your love for them is conditional. Your child will live their life in anxiety, believing that you will stop loving them if you don't approve of their actions or life choices. Doing this to your child will also lower their confidence and self-esteem. They may also develop codependency tendencies, leading to involvement in abusive relationships.

# How a Parent Can Help a Teen with Anxiety

As hard as it may be, one of your duties as a parent is to help your child navigate through all sorts of hardships. If you have a child with anxiety, you probably realize the magnitude of the issue. Knowing that your teen is struggling with all of these thoughts and emotions can be greatly disheartening. However, you must know that anxiety is very common, especially during the teen years. As a parent, you must teach your teen that anxiety management is a very important life skill. Everyone gets anxious at some point, though the intensity of the emotions differs. Luckily, there are multiple ways you can help your child manage their anxiety.

## Facing Anxiety

One of the best ways to deal with anxiety is learning how to face it. When you are anxious, you have no other option than to live through these tormenting emotions. Since anxiety disorders are frightening, learning how to tackle the situation is a great help. When attempting to help a teen with anxiety, you must listen and acknowledge their fears and understand that their thoughts and emotions are valid even when they don't sound that grave or realistic to you. Take your child seriously and offer them the support they need. Encourage them to do the things that they're anxious about without pushing them too hard. Help them set small goals and avoid taking control of the situation. If your teen decides to avoid a certain activity because they're anxious, do not shame them for it. Help them manage their feelings or reassure them that they can manage them in the future.

## Exploring Feelings

Most of the time, people who suffer from anxiety don't know what they're anxious about exactly. If your teen gets anxious all of a sudden, help them to break down their emotions. Walking them through recent events to identify the trigger also helps. It will help them understand their feelings and, ultimately, manage their anxiety, allowing them to avoid such situations in the future.

## Love and Support

Teens who suffer from anxiety can feel burdensome. They realize that they're not easy to deal with, which is also something that adds to their distress. Show your child constant love and support, as this helps them cope with their anxiety better. Set a good example for your child by managing your stress and anxiety.

# Calming an Anxious Child

Before exploring emotions, you must, first, calm your child down. Coming up with distractions or offering to engage in a fun activity can help them feel at ease. You can also practice deep breathing together or use the grounding method. If possible, take them for a walk or a run since fresh air can help them calm down.

Teenagers are at a high risk of developing mental disorders, such as anxiety and depression. Such illnesses are not easy to deal with and are stigmatized in several societies. People who don't have anxiety often find it hard to understand or acknowledge an anxious person's thoughts and emotions. However, if you are the parent of an anxious child, you must learn how to navigate this hardship with them.

# CHAPTER 5:

# WHAT TO DO IF MY TEEN HAS ANXIETY?

By now, you should clearly understand and decipher the signs related to anxiety, stress, and related mental health issues. This chapter will divide the common signs of anxiety based on selective characteristics to help you seek medical help and treatment options accordingly. By the end of this chapter, you will be able to recognize and treat anxiety-related signs, manage the situation, and take immediate action before it worsens.

## Common Signs of Anxiety

Even though we discussed the most prominent signs of anxiety in the previous chapter, we can further understand the symptoms in detail by categorizing them for easier diagnosis. The common signs of anxiety can be interpreted through emotional, physical, and behavioral phenomena.

## Emotional Signs of Anxiety

### Feeling on Edge

The continuous racing thoughts and feeling irritated are signs that your child is "feeling on edge." They may also not be able to address their feelings and emotions, let alone share them with others. Common signs of feeling on edge include emotional distress and being burned out. The constant guilt of not finishing tasks and the inability to begin working on them make your teen feel even more distressed, leading to this feeling of being on edge. If your teen freaks out when they think or talk about the future and their dreams, they may need help eliminating these feelings. It often leads the person to cause self-harm and hurt themselves.

## Constant Mood Swings

Do not mistake constant mood swings with hormonal changes. While hormones may play a major role in affecting your teen's mood, feeling the same way for a longer period can indicate a more serious health issue. Withdrawal symptoms, substance use, and anxiety disorders are often responsible for shifts in a teen's mood. Some mood disorders that teens are exposed to include bipolar disorder, major depressive disorder (MDD), disruptive mood dysregulation disorder (DMDD), cyclothymic disorder, personality disorder, and dysthymia. However, not all are related to anxiety, and they may have similar signs, making it difficult to diagnose the actual issue.

## Continuous Restlessness

If your teen sways from one place to another and refuses to settle in one place, they can be deemed restless. It often results from constant worrying and feeling nervous about their situation. Even though it might not necessarily be bad or harmful, your anxious teen may second-guess themselves and make it harder for them to accept reality. Another reason that can cause restlessness is the constant fear of bad things happening, even if they are less likely to occur. If your teen often thinks about the future and fears failing or not excelling at what they do, they may suffer from restlessness and anxiety.

## How to Treat Emotional Signs of Anxiety

An effective way to treat emotional signs that occur due to anxiety is journaling or keeping a diary. Encourage your child to keep a diary and write down their thoughts without feeling hesitant. Not all teens will be willing to document their thoughts on paper, but encouraging them will stimulate their brain. Provide the assurance of letting them keep their diary locked up. The assertion on privacy will motivate them to try this tactic. The idea is to decode a pattern of the teen's emotional journey and mood changes on a day-to-day basis.

As soon as your teen experiences signs of irritability or a major mood swing, ask them to note it down in their diary. Ask them to continue noting down their changes in feelings, mood, and thoughts over 2 weeks to cipher a pattern. With time, your child will be able to deduce signs of negative feelings and be prepared to face them instead of being anxious and panicking. Ask them to jot down positive feelings, too, as it will help them rate their irritability on a scale of 0 to 10.

The things and feelings that caused supreme anxiety can then be recognized as "triggers." This exercise may seem simple, but it is extremely effective as part of early diagnosis.

## Physical Warning Signs of Anxiety

### 1. Stomach and Gastrointestinal Issues

Anxiety and gastrointestinal issues are closely linked. Patients with recurring stomach issues are often checked for anxiety disorders and depression because any issue related to the abdomen and stomach is known to increase stress. It is also believed that the condition of the gut can impact stress levels. Prominent signs, such as trouble digesting food, diarrhea, constipation, abdominal cramps, and nausea, are commonly witnessed when suffering from gastrointestinal and stomach problems. Do not ignore these signs as they can be related to more serious anxiety disorders, such as panic disorder, social anxiety disorder (SAD), or phobia.

### 2. Sudden Weight Changes

As discussed in the previous chapter, sudden changes in body weight are also signs of anxiety and can be related to mental health issues. If your child has recently undergone excessive weight gain or loss, get them checked to detect the actual cause. Since they experience major hormonal changes during puberty, bodily changes are also common. However, if you see different signs related to weight issues, such as excessive eating, binge eating, changes in eating patterns, etc., in your teens, then monitor their food and eating habits. Since anxiety and eating disorders are closely related, watching what your teen eats and offering help is of the utmost importance.

## 3. Migraines

People suffering from stress and anxiety are also likely to experience headaches and migraines. While suffering from a headache once in a while shouldn't be a major concern, pay attention to your teen's condition if they frequently complain about recurring headaches. If a teenager has been addicted to alcohol, cigarettes, or drugs, they may also experience withdrawal symptoms when quitting. Relevant signs include a racing heart, restlessness, and headaches. In extreme cases, seeking medical help can alleviate symptoms and reduce stress levels in your teen. You can also consider the option of placing them in rehab if the situation gets out of control. At times, your teen may feel muscle spasms or pains as the body gets extremely tense in stressful situations.

Researchers also claim that prolonged anxiety-related issues can cause serious health issues, such as back and vision problems and even asthma.

## How to Treat Physical Signs of Anxiety

The simplest way to alleviate anxiety symptoms that physically affect your teen is by focusing on improving their physical endurance and incorporating changes to enhance body image. Begin with a daily, slow-paced, 30-minute walk early in the morning. Walking outside is highly recommended as it allows your teens time to reflect on their thoughts and put them together. It is also an effective relaxation technique that can help calm your child's mind. With time, encourage them to join aerobics or Pilates classes as this will also treat and train your child's muscles and relieve tension in delicate parts. In a nutshell, being active and focusing on physical movements will divert their attention and reduce stress.

When it comes to treating rapid breathing or the inability to breathe, teach some effective breathing techniques to your teen to cope with the situation instantly. It will prevent them from developing major breathing issues like asthma and calm their senses within a jiffy. Regulating proper sleep is also important as stress and improper sleeping patterns are closely related. Ensure that your teen has at least 7 to 8 hours of sound sleep. It will significantly improve their physical and mental health.

## Behavioral Manifestations of Anxiety

### 1. Procrastination

Another recurring effect of anxiety is procrastination, feeling lost, and the inability to concentrate. Staying restless and experiencing recurring negative thoughts leads to distraction, which eventually leads to procrastination. As you know, a teen with an anxiety disorder is highly likely to be lethargic and will keep delaying their tasks due to the fear of failing. Even though the task may take just a few hours to complete, your anxious teen may keep delaying it for weeks or even months.

### 2. Poor Performance

Lacking focus and procrastinating eventually leads to poor performance in school and resulting in low grades. Regularly skipping school also affects your teen's performance. Ensure they attend classes and feel at ease when they're studying or preparing for their tests. Skipping school and getting low grades are also related to the physical changes and anxiety of your teen. If they are sick and unable to complete tasks on time, do their homework, and study, they may have a major downfall of scores, diminishing their chance of getting into a reputed university. Since your teen's high school years are crucial for university entry, they must be pushed back on track.

## 3. Fear of Staying in Public or Alone

Teens with anxiety either need someone by their side in public places or stay completely isolated. While the former situation may stem from issues like separation anxiety, the latter is a result of social phobia. They will avoid meeting people and stay isolated in their rooms. Even if they go out, they need someone to accompany them in heavily crowded places. Their fear of meeting and talking to people may be misunderstood as rude or awkward behavior. In extreme cases, frequent outbursts are also commonly witnessed by parents. Teens embarrassed with this behavior may turn to compulsive behaviors, such as cleaning, frequent organization, arranging their books until they are satisfied, washing their hands every few hours, etc.

When left untreated, these physical, emotional, and behavioral signs can steadily become a serious issue that is difficult to cure in the long run.

## How to Treat Behavioral Signs of Anxiety

Taking some time out to reflect on important thoughts helps alleviate behavioral manifestations related to anxiety. Simple activities, such as listening to music, reading a book, or sipping tea, can calm the mind and provide enough energy to face reality. Encourage your teen to speak up and openly communicate their thoughts and emotions without feeling hesitant. Talk to your child's teacher and prepare a plan based on the signs they display. Since teachers observe and react to different behavioral signs daily, they can help you formulate an effective plan and appropriate treatment for your teen's anxiety.

Based on these categories that define distinct characteristics of anxiety, you can seek help accordingly. While some teens may experience anxiety emotionally, others will display varied behavioral signs.

## Common Treatment Options for Anxiety

Once you recognize the signs and comprehend that your teen is suffering from anxiety, take them for a clinical diagnosis, too. Apart from the common coping mechanisms and early diagnosis of anxiety at home, several treatment options are available that can be extremely helpful to treat your child's anxiety and prevalent symptoms.

### Breathing and Relaxation Techniques

Breathing techniques are extremely helpful to recover from an anxiety attack instantly. Since the frequency of anxiety attacks varies from person to person, performing breathing exercises reduces the symptom's chances of getting too serious. An anxious person's body is prone to being in a hyperventilation mode, and it can lack consistent flow and oxygen supply, which will worsen the situation as carbon dioxide is known to assist the body's anxious mode. Some may even show signs of shallow over-breathing.

Learning the correct breathing techniques, a teen can switch to breathing from their diaphragm instead of their chest, which helps them calm down within a few minutes. When you breathe in, let your belly expand.

One hand should be placed on the chest and the other on the lower abdomen.

This breathing technique, known as the abdominal breathing technique, is commonly used to treat anxiety and calm the senses. However, several techniques can be considered based on the teen's condition and severity of anxiety. The idea is to take in more oxygen and control its movements throughout the body while expelling carbon dioxide to alleviate stress. The involuntary functions monitored by the body's nervous system understand the deliberate attempt at controlling its breathing pattern and reduces stress. Along with feeling calmer, the body also experiences lower lactic acid levels, improved energy, and proper heart rate.

Mindfulness practices keep your anxious teen's recurring thoughts in control and help them concentrate. Since most teens are troubled due to anxious thoughts affecting their studies, mindfulness significantly alleviates the symptoms. Several exercises related to mindfulness and improved concentration levels can be useful for your teen. Guided imagery, meditation, and visualization techniques are some forms of mindfulness practices that relieve signs of anxiety. You can also try certain isometric relaxation techniques for your teen with the help of an expert.

**Cognitive-Behavioral Therapy**

This form of therapy is directed towards anxious individuals who cannot gather and face their thoughts, often leading to restlessness and feeling lost. Cognitive therapy uses tools and measures to change a teen's way of thinking and remolding their thought process to cope with stress. In essence, the negative feelings associated with anxiety, also known as triggers, can be effectively overcome with cognitive-behavioral therapy. Most of the time, such triggers make the anxiety worse and can push your teen into a downward spiral. For example, if your teen is suffering from social anxiety and no one pays attention to what they say, they will immediately think they are boring or worthless. This negative thought of feeling worthless is the trigger that can be treated or, at least, mellowed with the help of cognitive therapy.

Some of the impactful strategies and tools that make cognitive therapy useful are cognitive restructuring, attention training, rational, cognitive challenging, and encouraging self-talk. Exposure therapy is the primary strategy used in behavior therapy, helping the teen face their fears and acknowledge them. Since the inability to face fears and ignore them is one reason that triggers negative feelings, eradicating them is the easiest way to overcome this issue. The teen is asked to rank their fears in order of the worst to the least frightening thought and acknowledge each and every part of it.

Even though no actual medical test can firmly and dedicatedly diagnose anxiety, some effective screening tools help you understand your teen's condition and measure the level of anxiety they are facing. Experienced psychologists, counselors, and psychiatrists are well-versed with such screening techniques, which is why you must take your teen for an early screening test and start treatment as soon as possible.

## Counseling and Self-Help Group

Talking to a loved one and sharing your thoughts can also help. However, getting your teenage son or daughter to share their thoughts can be a difficult task. In such cases, seek help from counseling and self-help groups directed towards teens who feel worthless and fear meeting new people. It is an effective way to treat social phobia and improve communication skills. In essence, counseling sessions and self-help groups help your child get back on track by building their confidence and self-esteem.

Other signs such as constantly feeling depressed, experiencing mood swings, feeling shameful, etc., can be treated by participating in self-help groups. Some take help from strategies such as structured problem solving, which helps resolve procrastination and puts worrying thoughts at bay. Instead of focusing on what can go bad, your anxious teen will learn to direct their energy towards completing delayed tasks.

## Medication

Anxiety is also treated with medication, specifically in extreme situations like recurring anxiety attacks and when the teen has undergone episodes of self-harm. Medication is also considered when therapy hasn't or isn't working for the patient. Even though therapy works most of the time, people diagnosed with a higher level of anxiety may need to take medication along with consistent visits to their psychologist. A set of antidepressants and tranquilizers is often prescribed to patients who suffer from physical issues due to anxiety. Medical practitioners still advise them to undergo therapy to overcome anxiety in the long run.

## Physical and Dietary Changes

You can also establish certain physical and dietary lifestyle changes to reduce anxiety-related symptoms. Apart from physical benefits, exercising can boost mental health and treat psychological issues. By introducing effective changes in your teen's diet, you can control their hormone levels and balance cortisol and adrenaline levels. These hormones are responsible for changes in breathing patterns and heartbeat range, and feeding the right type of food can steadily treat the problem.

It is believed that a deficiency of magnesium, calcium and Vitamin B can heighten anxiety and depression-related signs. Monitoring the diet based on these supplements then becomes crucial. Certain food items, such as caffeine, salt, and nicotine, should be avoided as they trigger negative emotions. To achieve faster and safe results, consult a certified nutritionist and fitness trainer to customize a diet and exercise plan based on your teen's condition.

**Key Takeaway:** Anxiety can affect your teen's physical, mental, and emotional health majorly. As you know by now, if you fail to treat anxiety-related symptoms at the earliest, they will worsen and turn into depression or even bipolar disorder. Early diagnosis is possible by looking deep into the signs that your teen displays. Use certain tricks at home to help your teen cope with their issues. If the signs are too serious and untreatable at home, seek help from a therapist and encourage your teen to undergo treatment before it's too late. More importantly, make them feel safe and provide the assurance of staying by their side at all times.

The upcoming chapters will look into treatment options and coping mechanisms in detail to help you get a clearer idea and deal with the issue more adequately.

# CHAPTER 6:

# LEARN ABOUT AND TEACH ANXIETY

It is time to face reality and talk to your teen about what and how they are feeling. This chapter talks about your approach and communication skills when confronting your teen to make them feel at ease and reduce stress. While you do certain things for your anxious teen, you should refrain from uttering specific words and statements as they depreciate their vantage point. It's about being calm, supportive, and affirmative about your child's condition and keeping them assured. As you know by now, there is no right or straightforward approach to treat anxiety. All you can do is respond smartly to help your child cope with the stress and anxiety symptoms lucratively.

## Talking to Your Teen about Anxiety

### Talking about Fears and Worries

A supportive and patient parent can help treat a teen's anxiety at a faster and steady pace. If your teen is going through a hard time, show them your support and be open to discussion sessions. Be empathetic and compassionate towards your teen, especially when they approach you during a commotion. Do not scold them when they make a mistake. Instead, learn more about the triggers that could have led them to make a mistake.

Here are some questions you can ask your anxious teen to show your support.

- What thoughts do you often get?

- Are you worrying about something? Do you think I can help you with it?

- How are you feeling physically and mentally?

- Are you getting proper sleep?

- Are you eating properly? What foods and drinks do you often crave?

- What is bothering you?

- Is bullying common in your school? Has someone bullied you?

- Are you facing any fears? Are you scared of something?

- Are your friends supportive?

Regularly asking these questions helps you understand your child better and encourages you to design a pattern of their thought process. It not only makes diagnosis easier but also keeps your teen slightly at ease.

Utter words and statements like,

- I understand that the way you feel is terrible.

- I am here for you.

- Do not let your thoughts define you.

- We can get through this.

- You can talk to me about it openly.

- I promise to listen without judgment.

- The situation sounds intense, but you managed it well.

- You are doing your best.

- I care about you deeply.

These pep talk statements are converted into empathetic expressions that are more relatable to your teen. For example, instead of saying, "Be courageous" or "Buck up," be more empathetic and say, "I am extremely sorry you've been going through this" or "being in this state must feel terrible." Such paradoxes provide the reassurance of someone being truly understanding and supportive. Your teen will feel at ease and gather the courage to overcome the situation.

However, converting or reframing your words is not always an effective way to calm your teen. It may not work at all. In such cases, turn to a more realistic non-threatening way to help your child keep up. For example, go for a walk together or spend some time doing things that your child likes. You can also suggest meditation or take Pilates classes together.

## Delving Into the World of Anxiety

Initially, you may find your child being too sensitive or stubborn. However, once you delve into the world of anxiety and learn its true connotation, you will unravel the actual dilemma they are facing. When facing unwanted situations, they are just responding through the "fight-flight-freeze" trigger. Just like animals react to unwanted or dangerous circumstances by screeching or attacking the hunter, teens also often throw tantrums or outbursts as a coping mechanism.

In some cases, teens cannot cipher the actual degree of risk and why they get confused or feel lost. They may be unable to tell how dangerous a particular situation is or whether or not it is harmful. They may also rely on their parents to help them understand what they are going through. When they fail to get the support or help they are unconsciously expecting, their anxiety levels increase. As we have been emphasizing throughout this book, your duty as a parent is to recognize the signs, help your child overcome them, and be patient and supportive throughout this ordeal.

## **Identifying Anxiety**

The generation gap between you and your child is wide, and the mindsets are entirely different. You have to understand your child's mindset and dig deeper to perceive their world and situation through their perspective. Acknowledge that your child hates being clingy, stubborn, restless, or falling off the stairs. It is their nervousness and fidgety nature that their anxiety disorder has fathered.

Here is what you need to know about anxiety to help your teen.

> - Anxiety is not threatening. Many parents freak out when learning that their teenage child is going through anxiety. If your teen has recently been diagnosed with anxiety, you must know that it can be treated with patience and time. Everyone, at some point in their life, is prone to experiencing anxiety. It's important to understand that early diagnosis and treatment can alleviate relevant symptoms before it turns into a serious problem. However, it is not as dangerous as others claim. Still, it does not mean you can take the matter lightly.

- Anxiety is your body's way of preparing you. As discussed earlier, anxiety is common among people who sense danger around them. In other words, it is your body's way of preparing you to face the fear or danger around you. In some cases, random bursts of anxiety may help your teen perform at their best. However, it shouldn't be experienced for a prolonged period.

- Anxiety can become a problem when it interferes with your teen's day-to-day life. If your teen's anxiety is not allowing them to enjoy the simple pleasures of life or even finish their tasks with ease, it should not be taken lightly. With time, it can turn into distress. Situations like seeing a big dog approaching them or being separated from you for long can easily freak them out. They may also be seen screaming, obsessively biting their nails, picking their hair, or feeling unwell before or during important occasions.

## What Not to Do

While being with your anxious teen and supporting them at all times is of the utmost importance, there are certain things that you shouldn't say to them as it can make things worse. Dealing with anxiety is already nerve-wracking for your anxious teen, so saying certain things can create a negative image and phantasm that is difficult to exit. Even though the truth may be harsh to face at this point, it is always better than lying to your teen. Amusingly, the parents who have been through anxiety or are quite rational are the ones who may spit out the wrong words. Since they are more open-minded and practical, they are expected to say the right things and support their child correctly, which is not often the case. The chances of unconsciously dismissing their child's opinions are rather high than targeting the right pool of thoughts.

Here are some things that you should never say to your anxious teen.

## It's Not a Big Deal

Stop saying, "Don't sweat it" or "It's not a big deal" to your anxious teen because it actually is something huge and intense that they're going through. Even if it feels like a small issue from your perspective, it may not be as dainty as you think. Instead of illustrating it as a positive or uplifting message, your teen may feel worse since the problem doesn't seem as huge to someone else. It is known that people suffering from anxiety and related symptoms feel things more intensely. For them, every emotion and thought is too big and vehement. Instead of being contradictory, enter and feel your teen's belief system and take an encouraging step instead of demeaning their viewpoint. If you acknowledge the intensity of the situation, you can successfully help your anxious teen. Validate their thoughts by telling them they can do it and handle the situation with courage, just like they did it in the past.

## Stop Worrying, Or There's Nothing to Be Scared Of

Telling someone not to be worried when they are constantly exposed to worrying thoughts is unfitting and unreasonable. It's like putting a tiny bandage on a huge wound that is oozing pools of blood - in other words, it is useless and even demeaning in some cases. This form of reassurance can produce negative repercussions. Telling them not to be afraid of the future and incoming negative thoughts is useless and counter-intuitive. Since they have several fears, namely peer pressure, judgment, failure, not getting accepted, etc., telling them not to be afraid is meaningless. Instead, ask them what they fear the most and be open about confronting them. Instead of telling them "Don't worry" or "Stop worrying," ask them more about the nature of their worries and what you can do to cure them.

## I Feel Anxious Too

Don't try to relate and compare your situation with your child's condition. Even though you may be trying to calm them down by portraying your example and telling them everything will be okay, they may perceive it negatively. By pressing on your anxiety, you are unknowingly belittling their serious condition. If you, as a parent, aren't taking it seriously, your child will lose all hopes of overcoming the situation, too. Even though you may feel anxious, you should not convey it to your teen. As an adult, you have a better sense of control and maturity to handle stress and deploy effective coping mechanisms. However, your teenage daughter or son is still immature and trying to learn several things simultaneously. Comparing your anxiety with your child's is far from unacceptable. Moreover, stress and anxiety can be contagious, and you should never feed off each other's anxiety.

## You'll Be Fine

Telling them that they will be fine when they are clearly in a loop can be dangerous, too. Ignoring their heightened symptoms and shadowing them with a "You'll be fine" statement is a blatant lie. Your teen knows the true definition of "fine" is something that is way beyond their current situation and seems absurd. They believe that feeling fine is an overstatement, and they will never get to experience it. With a mind buzzing with thoughts and emotions and a heart that is constantly racing, your child will feel anything but fine. Your teen will not be fine until you take the matter seriously and take the necessary steps to treat them. Instead of saying that they will be fine, tell your troubled teen you will be there for them and help them with whatever they need.

## I'll Do It for You

Since most anxious teens keep putting off things and delaying tasks, step in to encourage them to finish their chores instead of doing it for them. It can turn into a habit in the long run, and your teen may start relying on you to complete the smallest tasks that they could have managed. Let them gather their thoughts and find the courage and enthusiasm to finish the pending tasks on their own. By doing so, you will give them enough space to face reality and motivate them to be independent. Even though most anxious teens wish to address their thoughts, adamant parents who want to fix things for their teens at the earliest will get in the way. It often leads to parents saying things like, "You can rest. I will finish it for you." If you make this a habit, your teen will fail to acknowledge the tasks they are loaded with, leading to deeper procrastination and eventually affecting their grades and sense of responsibility.

## You Need More Sleep

Many people with anxiety often resort to sleep as a coping mechanism. However, some may find it extremely difficult to sleep. They are constantly cited with anxious thoughts and negative emotions, leading to sleeping issues, other mental health issues, and even insomnia. Your teen may divert their anxiety and racing thoughts during the day by completing schoolwork or house chores. However, as the sun sets and the daily chaos submerges, their mind starts filling with worried thoughts about the future and the fear of failure making it difficult to sleep and causing restlessness. If all problems could be cured by sleep, everyone would be happy and carefree. You cannot tell them to sleep more if they cannot get even two to three hours of sleep in the first place. Instead, make them feel relaxed and suggest activities that induce sleep, such as meditation and aromatherapy.

**Stop Thinking**

Your anxious teen will not stop thinking if you simply ask them not to. Who wouldn't love to shut their racing thoughts and feel more relaxed? Naturally, it is not in their hands to stop thinking or worrying just because you mentioned it. Your teen may be caught up in a loop of negative and fearful thoughts, which are often difficult to overcome. If you cannot provide proper support, you won't break your child's thought cycle. Instead of asking your child to stop thinking, feed their brain with positivity and encouraging thoughts to balance out the negativity. Fill their mind with positive emotions to help them cope with the stressful thought process they are caught in. For example, if they are worried about failing their exams, do not tell them to shun such negative thoughts. Instead, motivate them by telling them how capable they are. Statements like, "You're worthy of achieving success" and "You can get into the college of your dreams" are some examples of positive reinforcement that your child needs to hear in their state of commotion.

## Can You Hurry Up?

Asking them to hurry up or just complete a task without causing a fuss is off the charts. Teens diagnosed with chronic anxiety are often burdened with poor decision-making skills and regretting their past decisions. Some even try to achieve perfection in everything they do, which slows their pace. If you ask them to do things faster or hurry up, they will either mess up their tasks or feel guiltier. Since they are already feeling helpless and fear being judged, they will resent their presence and the way they handle things. Instead of pressurizing them to move hastily, ask them if you can do anything to help. Since they are prone to feeling panicky and anxious when doing certain things, like boarding a plane or being in a crowded place, give them time to overcome their fears and gather their thoughts. With your support, they can steadily increase their pace with time. Until then, try to be as patient as possible.

## It's In Your Head

This is another statement that you should never utter in front of your anxious teen. These words are not only hurtful for your child but also represent your ignorant attitude. In a way, you are shaming your child by failing to acknowledge the real problem and blaming it on their brain. With time, your child will spiral into deeper pools of guilt and shame, after which pulling them out will be nearly impossible. Remember, your teen hasn't chosen to be in this state. If they could, they would have beaten this plight long ago. They still can if they have your support and the right insights to treat their condition. Word your sentences carefully when dealing with such situations. For example, a statement like, "Your worried brain is hyperactive and needs some rest. Why don't we get some ice cream and discuss your thoughts on our way?" can be very effective.

## I Don't Understand What You Need

Supervising and taking care of an anxious teen can be confusing and exhausting. At times, you may not know what they want and why they behave in a certain way. It can be even more frustrating when your child is unwilling to talk to you and throws tantrums as a coping mechanism. However, you cannot take it out on your child. Even if you don't understand what your teen needs, you should not convey your ambiguity. Instead, talk to them and understand their thought process. Deep down, your child wants you to be supportive, patient, and calm, especially when they are hyperactive and caught in a loop. By displaying feelings of confusion and hopelessness, your child will feel even more lost and nervous. If you, as a parent, portray signs of failure, what is your child supposed to do?

**Key Takeaway:** Even though you may feel that you are a well-meaning and attentive parent, you may accidentally utter certain statements that heighten the negative anxiety symptoms in your teen instead of mellowing them down. Yes, it is difficult for you to see your child in their worst condition, but you shouldn't lose hope. Be supportive, say the right things, and provide the assurance of always being there for your child. Do not verbalize negative thoughts. Instead, learn the right way to deal with such intense situations. At times, listening to them with an open mind instead of uttering words of encouragement is more helpful. It also diminishes the chances of saying something unacceptable by accident. More importantly, every parent should stay calm and be affirmative to keep their child reassured.

## CHAPTER 7:

# STRATEGIES TO SUPPORT AN ANXIOUS TEEN

By this point in the book, you have probably grasped a better idea of your teen's anxiety and understand that supporting them will not be a walk in the park. Before you try to help them, you must be fully aware that anxiety is highly unpredictable. You should also anticipate that the healing process will not be quick or predictable. It will usually feel like you and the child that you want to help are trying to navigate through a raging sea. No matter how understanding and compassionate they are, many parents who are determined to help their anxious children can easily lose their temper. Dealing with anxiety, more often than not, is a very frustrating experience for anyone involved. Regardless of how hard they try, no one who has never suffered from anxiety can wrap their head around the reality of this disorder. Many people tend to underestimate anxiety and its symptoms, although they may know a lot about how it works.

To most people, anxiety is a sign of weakness and is a reflection of a person's resilience, courage, and character. However, this couldn't be further from the truth. At first glance, anxiety seems like worry and fear of certain situations, and while this is true to an extent, it barely scratches the surface of anxiety. People who have anxiety are among the strongest people, and they regularly encounter and push themselves to the limit in various situations where they feel uncomfortable and anxious. You may get the idea that anxious teens are baffled and lost, though they are usually the first to come up with a practical solution in times of danger. The chances are that they have lived through numerous variations of the same situation in their minds and identified the different outcomes. Anxiety can set off at any given moment, without any warning. It doesn't mean there is something wrong going on in their brain. It simply means that your anxious teen's brain is a little more overprotective or preoccupied. Anxiety doesn't define your child, nor is it a personality trait. It is a wave of intense emotions that comes and goes.

Anxious brains are very strong and can feel impossible to fight against. They are persuasive and pervasive, and they will leave your child with negative thoughts and excessive worry. Its strength can trigger other disorders, such as OCD and panic disorders. Anxiety will leave your child feeling out of control, isolated, worried, afraid, and overwhelmed. It also comes with numerous physical symptoms, including nausea, tense muscles, tightness in the chest, and dizziness. It is often exhibited in behavioral symptoms like nail-biting and hair and skin picking. Anxiety is a very difficult battle to take on. Therefore, this book discusses strategies in detail to help you support an anxious teen.

## Set Realistic Expectations

### Setting Expectations

One of the most important things to do when you decide to jump right in and support an anxious teen is to set clear and realistic expectations. As discussed above, anxiety- whether it's at its peak or controlled -

is very mysterious. Regardless of whether you aim to help a teen entirely recover from their anxiety or just wish to help them fight the occasional battle, it will not be a smooth ride. Anticipating the best is very easy, especially when you are close to the child you're trying to help. It may be because you believe that you can help them, expect to get to them faster, presume that they are willing to accept your help or respond to your support, or simply wish to believe that they will feel better soon. However, approaching the situation with nothing but positivity can set you up for disappointment, but you both under more pressure, leave your teen feeling guilty, and make you feel bad for being unable to help them. You must remember that for your support to work, the effort needs to be two-way. They need to be fully willing to accept your help and not succumb to their anxiety. It's good to hope for the best, and it is recommended that you do so but don't set very high expectations. There are also times where you will feel like you are doing better, but don't get ahead of yourself and remember that it's not all sunshine and rainbows.

## Don't Make It Personal

Understandably, you want your teen to defeat their anxiety and fears. Many parents believe that their children are capable of achieving so much and that anxiety is holding them back from unlocking their full potential. However, sharing those beliefs with someone with anxiety makes things worse for them. Pushing them to fight harder and imposing your help can be very distressing. Forcing a teen to face specific situations before they're ready is very counterproductive, leading to more psychological problems. You must prepare yourself for the worst as they may not feel prepared just yet, and may not even accept your support, to begin with. It doesn't mean that you should give up on them, and don't take their rejection personally either. You have to constantly remind yourself that the entire situation is not about you. These are not your fears, you are not the one facing them, and it is not up to you to decide when and how their anxiety should be tackled. You are a support figure - you are helping your teen out of love and compassion. It is not a mission - you are dealing with vulnerable human emotions. You merely need to be patient, listen to them, and take it at their pace.

**Accepting Help**

Being there for your teen even when they are not the easiest to deal with will eventually lead them to open up to you and give in to your support. People with anxiety don't choose how they feel, and even their rejection of your support can be a product of their anxiety. It's not easy for them to accept or ask for help. The thoughts and feelings accompanied by anxiety sometimes feel too personal. Other emotions and thoughts may be extremely intense, to the point where they feel terrified to explore. Many teens who have anxiety also deliberately associate it with their identity. They may feel afraid to explore who they are without the anxiety factor. These are all things that may cause them to push you away and capitulate to their anxiety.

## What Are You Avoiding?

Supporting someone with anxiety is very tricky. If you've never been in the situation, you won't truly be able to tell what your anxious teen would and wouldn't like to hear. There are many phrases or words that you may think are reassuring and helpful, but in reality, they undervalue an anxious person's emotions and make them feel misunderstood. On the other hand, there are several things you may feel like you should avoid doing or saying when they are actually very helpful.

## Discussing Thoughts and Emotions

Many people avoid talking about an anxious teen's emotions and focus on making them laugh or lighten up the mood instead. When dealing with an anxious child, don't avoid discussing their thoughts and feelings. Emotions and ideas are the core of anxiety - when you don't tackle the main issue, it may seem like you would rather do something more fun rather than listening to the child. While you may be doing this purely out of good intentions, your teen may feel like they are burdensome or boring. It will prevent them from discussing their worries with you in the future. Besides, a good laugh is a temporary fix. Meanwhile, delving into the main problem helps your teen gain clarity and helping them when they're in similar situations.

## Encouraging Therapy

You may think that encouraging therapy or supporting them to seek professional help is insulting. You may be surprised to learn that many teens with psychological disorders wish to have someone willing to support them throughout this journey. Many teens wish to seek professional support but are afraid. If you change the subject when they bring up therapy or reluctantly talk about it, you may be unintentionally encouraging the stigma. Don't push them to see a therapist, but instead, ask them how they feel about seeing one. Explain to them why you think this may be a good idea and offer to help them find a professional with whom they feel comfortable. Offer to go with them and stay in the waiting room until they finish. If they feel overwhelmed, ask if they would like you to help them plan what they want to talk to the therapist about. Don't make them feel like they need to tell you what went on during the session, as they will tell you if they feel comfortable enough.

## Looking After Yourself

Helping someone with a mental illness is a great challenge, and just like you may feel the need to look after them, you must look after yourself. You may tell yourself that now is not the time to make time for yourself or that they need your help more than you need looking after. However, you need to remember that overloading yourself affects your mental health, too. Keep in mind that no matter the type of relationship you have with your teen, you are not responsible for diminishing their anxiety. Besides, you have to help yourself before you can help them. Only focusing on the anxious adolescent will eventually make you unable to support them, in the same way, any longer. If you notice that you have started feeling unwell, it is time to set boundaries. Determine how much help you can offer and your limits. If possible, have someone else support them during the process so that not all of the weight falls on you. As long as you don't share with others information about your teen's issues, you are allowed to talk to others about how you are feeling. You need the support as well.

**Worrying Isn't Bad**

As someone who is deeply involved in anxiety's complexities, you can be led to believe that "worry" is a nemesis. This belief can be very harmful to you and the child you are trying to help. Believing that worrying, in general, is a bad thing causes problems for you later on. It also promotes toxic positivity, making you feel like you need to force a positive mindset even when things get very hard. There is a difference between excessive worry and obsessing over the tiniest details to the point of an anxiety disorder and worrying in alarming or drastic situations. People with anxiety disorders worry about things as simple as walking over to the garbage can during a meeting or class. They will replay the situation several times in their mind and think about multiple ways of how this scenario can play out. Worrying to this extent is unhealthy. However, worrying is a normal human function and is what makes us human. If you don't worry, you will not develop a defense strategy or trigger a fight or flight response in dangerous situations. If you don't worry about your health, you won't maintain healthy habits. If you don't worry about relationships, you will not make an effort to maintain them and end up losing many friends - the list goes on. This is what you should explain to your child precisely. Make it clear that you are trying to combat unhealthy worry and not worry as a concept.

**Anxiety Coping Kit**

Anxiety is like a ticking time bomb. It can go off anywhere at any time. Meaning, that no matter how close you are to the teen with anxiety, you can't guarantee that you'll be there every time they feel anxious. Even if you are worried for them, you can't constantly monitor or accompany them wherever they go. However, it's always good to be prepared. There are many ways to deal with anxiety, and creating an anxiety coping kit is one of them. An anxiety coping kit is a collection of various physical items, activities, notes, and reminders. Since each teen experiences anxiety differently, offer to create their coping kit with them or gather as much information about their thoughts, feelings, symptoms, and behavior when their anxiety kicks in before creating it for them.

An effective anxiety coping kit can include a written note that reminds them to take 10 deep breaths as this helps ease hyperventilation and shortness of breath. A note that reminds them to use the 54321 grounding technique will also be of great help. Ask them to name 5 things they can see, think of 4 things they can feel on their body, listen to 3 sounds, name 2 things they can smell, and 1 thing they can taste. If they have a prescribed inhaler for their panic or anxiety attacks, ensure to include it in the kit. Many teens experience digestive issues or loss of appetite with their anxiety, so include their favorite snack bar or a protein shake to ensure they still get healthy nutrition. Include a small notebook and a pencil since writing their feelings down helps them gain insight and express their emotions. If your teen sees a therapist, encourage them to take the notebook with them to their following session. A note with a list of names and contact numbers of people they can reach out to is important to include as hearing a loved one's voice can be very soothing. Make sure to include a small activity, such as an adult coloring book, a fidget toy or cube, or a Rubik's cube, to keep them occupied. This prevents them from exhibiting harmful behavioral symptoms. Write a letter to your child, or ask them to write a letter to themself and include it in the kit. The letter can be a list of things they're good at, things they're passionate about, and what they love about themselves, their affirmations, or even a reminder that their current situation is temporary. Though it is not portable, a weighted blanket helps soothe their anxiety if they're at home. It will make them feel guarded, secure, and safe. Add a funny memory or picture to give them something to smile about. Laughter can lower your teen's cortisol levels, which are responsible for stress hormones. Ask them to write down their blessings or things they're grateful for and include the note in the kit.

## Reframing Anxious Thoughts

Reframing anxiety is a process that allows anxious teens to reinterpret an experience, situation, or event. This technique allows them to change the way they perceive something and, therefore, change how they feel about it. Reframing can help them overcome their anxiety and is completed through a simple process. The next time your teen feels anxious, ask them to write down the problem or situation, followed by their thoughts regarding it. Then, ask them to write down how they feel about it. Afterward, the reformation process begins. Ask them to write 4 alternative thoughts to the situation. For instance, if they're worried about trying out a new sport, the alternative thoughts could look like the following: if they ended up hating it, at least they found out how they feel about it, or if they liked it, but it's painful, then they are strengthening their muscles. The next step is listing evidence that supports the alternative thoughts they created. This can be personal evidence, such as evidence of personal growth. The final step is writing down how they feel after reframing their thoughts.

**Practice Empathy**

One of the most important things to do if you want to support your teen with anxiety is to practice empathy. You probably already feel compassion for them. However, many parents forget to express these feelings. It is important to stay strong for them and approach the situation strategically, though sometimes they prefer to know that someone understands how they feel. Instead of constantly providing them with solutions, practice making them feel validated and express concern.

## Concentrate On the Basics

Anxiety is not easy to deal with, and you might feel like you have to resort to complicated and drastic measures immediately. However, keep in mind that there is usually not much to do for your teen during the attack. Try to calm them down and ensure they feel safe. Practice breathing exercises with them, and once they start feeling better, you can start to explore their thoughts and feelings with them. Let them know that you are there for them, understand them, and want to help them.

Key Takeaway: Supporting a teen with anxiety may be one of the hardest things you'll ever have to do. Anxiety is a very complicated mental disorder. It constantly eats away at the teen's mind and may even cause them to reject help even when they need it. To help someone manage their anxiety, you must truly understand how they feel and how their thoughts are tied to these emotions. It's helpful to explore different coping techniques to find out which method is most effective. As long as you don't pressure them or overload yourself at the expense of supporting them, progress can be made.

# CHAPTER 8:

# SELF-SOOTHING TECHNIQUES FOR TEENS WITH ANXIETY

As discussed in the previous chapters, anxiety in the teenage years can be quite severe. While seeing a therapist can guide teens in the right direction, there are also plenty of exercises and techniques they can practice on their own to become mindful and to anchor themselves in the present moment. Self-soothing techniques should never be used as a cure but as a means to control thoughts in the conscious mind, and with time, train the subconscious to see the bigger picture. These techniques are recommended by certified psychotherapists and have proven to be an effective method to calm the mind and work on "resetting" the brain. This chapter covers the practices to help teens reduce stress and soften any feelings of anxiety that would otherwise snowball into a panic attack.

## Practices for Long-term Effects

### Acceptance

While it may sound counterproductive, psychotherapists advise teens to accept their anxiety as a self-preservative knee-jerk reaction to stressful situations. Anxiety is more understood as a disorder in this day and age, and teens must understand that there is no shame in their struggle and that they're not alone.

Feelings of anxiety can either be inherited, the result of a rough upbringing, or past traumas – but whatever the cause, its function is to signal the individual that they're in a state of danger. It can be a danger of failing, losing someone dear to them, or perceived belittlement or embarrassment. As mentioned in previous chapters, anxiety in teens can also be fueled by bullying at school or poor self-esteem. Accepting the cause and the outcome is the first step to treatment.

Psychotherapists claim that any attempt of suppressing shame will backfire and worsen anxiety. Therefore, it's advised for anxious teens to see a therapist regularly so that they can pinpoint any potential causes of their worries and work on resolving or accepting them.

**Yoga for Mindfulness**

An anxious mind wanders to the past or gets caught in a web of possible future scenarios, and working on anchoring oneself in the present moment is a crucial step toward a calmer mind, which is known as a state of mindfulness. Unfortunately, neurodivergent teens with attention disorders may find this practice more challenging than others, but it's not a challenge that they cannot overcome with dedication and support.

Teens can tell their Yoga instructors specifically why they're taking up the practice. This way, yoga poses that directly ease feelings of anxiety can be taught from the beginning. These poses include but are not limited to the tree pose, the extended triangle pose, the child's pose, the half-moon pose, the bridge pose, among others. Specific poses can easily be learned online, as they are quite easy to do and require nothing but a yoga mat.

## Aerobic Exercise

Although an active lifestyle should never be seen as the ultimate replacement for prescribed medication, countless studies prove the benefits of aerobic exercise in helping individuals manage common anxiety symptoms.

Traditionally, it was presumed that active lifestyles lead to a more positive body image and making individuals more confident. However, modern studies suggest that only five minutes of aerobic exercise per day can stimulate anti-anxiety effects. Some of these studies state that five to ten minutes is as effective as an intense 45-minute workout session.

When teens exercise, their bodies release "happy" hormones and chemicals, such as dopamine and other endorphins that stabilize the mood and regulate other hormones like serotonin. This not only impacts a teen's mood but also enables their brain cells to become more "active."

To reap the benefits of exercise, teens can go for a morning jog, do cardio at home, or get an exercise companion and go to the gym as part of a daily routine.

## Tai Chi

Also known as shadowboxing, Tai Chi is a Chinese martial art form commonly practiced for self-defense. However, it also incorporates mindfulness and meditation, making it a physical and a mental exercise. It is one of the most highly recommended practices for those who have anxiety.

Due to the nature of Tai Chi's relaxed and gentle motions, it effectively keeps stress at bay. Teens can sign up for classes online or at a martial art center. It's best to avoid free videos, as this form of martial arts is very particular and needs to be learned correctly and frequently performed to reap its myriad benefits.

Professional Tai Chi instructors teach breathing techniques and specific positions. Injuries are always a possibility if practiced incorrectly, so professional training is recommended.

Other benefits of Tai Chi include easing symptoms of depression, stabilizing the mood and preventing mood swings, increased stamina, better sleep quality, and reduced risk of joint pain, falls, and even heart failure.

## Deep Breathing

Deep breathing is a relatively simple and easy exercise to learn. It effectively combats anxiety and panic attacks, and the outcome is almost instantaneous. The exercise works by lengthening the exhale rather than the inhale. The teen doesn't need to fill their lungs with air completely as long as they inhale a deep breath and take their time letting the air out through their noses.

The trick is to work on belly breathing - lie down with one hand on the chest and the other on their torso, right above the belly button. They must then breathe in through the nose for three seconds, noticing how their belly rises as the lungs fill with air, and breathe out through the mouth very slowly for around six seconds. They need to repeat this exercise for at least ten minutes, as this trains the muscles to breathe in deeper, which has immediate and long-term anti-anxiety effects.

## Writing

Having a hobby helps teens relieve their overwhelming and worrying feelings by using an outlet to expend their negative and intrusive thoughts. Writing is a great exercise that helps teens pinpoint the root cause of their negative feelings. Whenever they find themselves in an anxious state, they can grab a pen and paper or use an electronic device to jot down what's on their minds.

While the exercise helps teens privately vent to themselves, writing in and of itself also allows the mind to focus on the act of writing rather than negative thoughts. This can last anywhere from a few minutes to an hour, and teens are advised to stop only when their anxiety has subsided.

It's best to designate time as part of a daily schedule to write. Incorporating this practice into routines trains the brain to identify problems and resolve them. Teens can present their writing to their therapist or legal guardian to help address their worries in a more practical approach and avoid these worries as potential panic triggers.

**Art Therapy**

Many types of art therapy are suitable for easing anxiety in teens. As previously discussed, having a hobby helps alleviate and soften symptoms. Studies have shown that these three types of art therapy are ideal for teens with anxiety disorders.

### • Slow Drawing

The teen doesn't need to be naturally good at drawing to take it up as a hobby. It's a skill that can be learned with time. Slow drawing, in particular, has shown promising results in easing feelings of worry as it's considered a meditative exercise. All the teen needs to slow-draw is a pencil and paper. The hand is moved at a slower pace than usual, which allows the teen to focus on nothing but the process they are performing. They can draw shapes, people, or even symbols of what's on their minds. This exercise can immediately calm the mind and clear all the negative thoughts.

### • Painting

Painting is hailed as an effective stress-reliever. Unlike slow painting, there is no particular technique that distinguishes it from painting as a leisure activity. Scientists believe that only 45 minutes of painting a day can boost a teen's confidence and keep anxiousness at bay.

Teens can sign up for painting classes or look for free online lessons. As an exercise, painting allows the teen to immerse themselves in the craft completely and focus on nothing but the piece they're working on. Studies also suggest that painting stimulates feel-good hormones like dopamine, potentially balancing a teen's brain chemicals, altering their behavior, thinking patterns, and reactions to different stimuli.

- **Clay Modeling**

What makes working with clay the perfect exercise for neurodivergent teens is its sensory benefits. With nothing but clay and their hands, teens get more in touch with their movements and bodies as they use their fingers to create art. Because it's a form of art that requires patience to master, this trains a teen's brain to "slow down" and, in turn, makes them less fidgety and much calmer with time.

## Techniques for Immediate Relief

While the previous exercises work on long-term results, there are quick practices that provide immediate calming effects that come in handy when the teen is on the brink of a panic or anxiety attack. These techniques can be practiced anywhere in public, but they most effectively provide relief when done in a quiet and comfortable space. An anxiety attack can be best described as a wave. Teens can guide their thoughts to a safe space until the wave passes. It's recommended they find a place where they can be alone for a few minutes before doing these exercises.

## Counting

It sounds like a very simplistic exercise, and it is. Counting is an easy and effective way to give the mind something to focus on other than feelings and thoughts of anxiety. Counting exercises are helpful for neurodivergent teens with autism or ADHD who find themselves on the brink of a meltdown.

In this exercise, the teen closes their eyes and begins to count to ten slowly. If they're more anxious than usual, they can count to a higher number, but it's advised to stop and start over. The individual keeps counting to give the mind something else to focus on until anxious feelings subside. Because anxiety is more severe in some teens than others, this exercise can provide immediate relief or take a few minutes longer to work.

The trick is to focus on nothing but counting and avoid thinking about whether the exercise is working. If the teen is in a private space, they can combine this exercise with slow breathing techniques and visualization.

Moreover, while counting is best known to give immediate results, it also trains the brain to be redirected to a state of mindfulness when stress accumulates. With time, teens can find even quicker relief in a shorter period when practicing the exercise.

**Confrontation**

Confronting negative thoughts can be challenging. If the teen is not properly trained on how to do this, it can backfire, so it's important to practice this with a therapist or at home under supervision before they practice it on their own. Anxiety is, in most cases, exacerbated by other mental illnesses and disorders that can alter the negative thoughts that pass through the teen's mind, including harmful and untrue presumptions that add fuel to the fire. Confrontation is, therefore, a great tool to nip the cause in the bud and calm the mind with logic rather than by distracting it. This exercise is most effective when anxiety is still developing, and it should never be practiced in an attempt to dissuade a rapidly approaching panic attack.

The exercise works by breaking the cycle before it begins, and this is done by having a mental conversation with one's self. The teen starts by visualizing their anxious thoughts as a projected version of themselves – one that they can converse with and calm down, and they start asking questions of what it is that's worrying them. If the teen is in an overstimulating environment, such as a loud party or a large social gathering, they need to find a quiet and comfortable place before they begin.

If thoughts of anxiety are caused by a tight deadline at school, a social relationship, or any situation they don't have control over, they can ask themselves what the worst-case scenario would be and accept and make peace with it. For instance, if the consequence they're thinking of is failing a class, they can think of a reassuring backup plan, especially one that is previously devised with their parents' help. Therefore, it's important for parents and therapists to go over every detail that might be worrying the teen.

On the flip side, if the anxiety is rooted in something they cannot change, such as the death of a pet or loved one or moving, the teen needs to do the opposite of mindfulness. Instead of anchoring themselves in the present moment, they look ahead to the future and find peace in what is to come.

It's important to note that this is not an exercise that can be improvised. The answers to the questions that the teen asks themselves must be pre-determined with the help of a therapist or a legal guardian. This exercise helps organize their thoughts and reminds them of the bigger picture.

**Correct Posture**

Psychotherapy studies show a behavioral pattern in teens when they are anxious. When approaching a state of panic, instinct kicks in and leaves them in fight-or-flight mode, which usually makes them hunch over to protect the upper body – where the heart and lungs are, making it difficult to snap out of an anxious state.

If the teen finds themselves in this posture, they need to correct it immediately. They're advised to stand, straighten their backs, and pull back their shoulders and their feet planted on the ground firmly.

The next step is to close their eyes and breathe through their noses as deeply as possible until their lungs are full before exhaling through the mouth slowly. When the posture is combined with breathing exercises, the muscles become less tense, and the brain realizes that it's not in danger and that it's, most importantly, in full control. This, in turn, affects passing thoughts and calms the mind. It's also believed that posture correction softens anxiety and helps teens have firmer control over it.

**Aromatherapy**

In case a teen feels anxious in the comfort of their home, they can use aromatherapy for its soothing effects, sometimes in combination with the previous exercises for quicker relief. Essential oils are no magic cure, but studies have proven their efficacy in calming the body and mind and relieving stress. Lavender oil is the most popular choice for this technique, but teens can also use tea tree, basil, or citrus oils if they prefer a particular scent.

These oils can be used in a dispenser for long-term effects, or teens can carry a dropper with them. A few drops on the wrist and the neck can help, but essential oils are most effective when added to a warm bath, as this helps muscles relax and allows space to perform breathing exercises. The oils can also be massaged on the temples, or a few drops can be added to body lotion. This technique is not effective in an impending panic attack but rather in keeping stress at bay.

**Herbal Teas**

Before the advent of pharmaceuticals, herbs were used to treat anxiety and depression. Herbal teas have soothing effects, but they should never be used as a replacement for prescribed medication.

There's a range of herbs that teens can safely consume to reap their calming benefits. They're quick and easy to brew and can help anxious teens have better quality sleep, especially when anxiety causes insomnia. Peppermint leaves or peppermint extract can be consumed to relieve anxiety, while its scent is soothing and also used for aromatherapy.

Chamomile is another great herb that helps calm the mind and muscles, and it's also a powerful anti-inflammatory. Because herbal teas have no caffeine content, there's practically no risk of overconsumption as long as refined sugar is not added. Studies suggest that long-term consumption of chamomile extract helps individuals control moderate to severe anxiety symptoms. Similarly, lavender is also a mood stabilizer and has sedative effects.

Another herb that can be consumed in tea is kava. It works by targeting GABA receptors, the part in the brain responsible for feelings of stress and worry. Although there's practically no risk of consuming these herbs, legal guardians should always consult the teen's physician before adding these natural remedies to their diets.

**Audio Therapy**

Music or audio therapy is a more experimental anti-anxiety technique. While it's scientifically proven that music releases endorphins and stabilizes moods, it's best used for short-term results and to relieve stress.

However, music therapy isn't simply having your teen listen to their favorite song. As suggested by anecdotal evidence, anti-anxiety audios, guided meditations, and so-called "subliminal" may provide immediate relief for some teens who struggle with frequent panic attacks.

Binaural beats and isochronic tones are usually embedded in these audio recordings. Usually categorized as "brainwave entrainment," these audio files contain two tones, each of a slightly different frequency. The small difference in the frequency is believed to trick the brain into hearing a third tone. It stimulates neurons in the brain to synchronize with this imaginary sound, which allegedly decreases anxiety and is even claimed to improve cognitive functions.

Some of these audio recordings that are barely audible may also embed positive affirmations in an attempt to bypass the conscious brain and plant these affirmations directly in the subconscious, which alters the teen's behavior over time. Although an experimental kind of therapy, some individuals report feeling more at ease overnight after listening to this music.

**Key Takeaway**: It's recommended to allow teens to choose the techniques and practices they're comfortable doing and to only follow up with their progress without pressuring them into doing more than what they have the energy for. Following several or all of the self-soothing techniques in this chapter will facilitate all areas of life, and not only a teen's state of mind. It's essential to stay consistent and to remember that results are accumulative and take time to show.

Psychotherapists recommend these practices, and if no significant progress is seen in a few weeks, parents must consult a certified psychotherapist who specializes in teen psychology.

# CHAPTER 9:

# TEENAGE SUICIDE

Taking one's own life is an extremely strenuous decision, which is taken after a person develops a thought pattern compelling them to cause harm and end their life. When a teen is willing to undergo a process or experience that is dangerous to them and causes physical harm, the phenomenon is known as suicidal ideation, and this is often accompanied by suicidal behavior and relevant pathogenesis.

If your teen seems to be at risk of committing suicide, you must take immediate action to combat the situation and prevent them from causing self-harm.

# Teens at Risk

## Teens Who Have Been through Trauma

Trauma is the most common cause or sign of risk in teens who have tried to commit suicide. While addiction and depression are the two main triggers that compel teens to commit suicide, traumatic experiences are also a major reason that put them at risk. Post-Traumatic Stress Disorder (PTSD) and Acute Stress Disorder (ASD) are the two common types of mental health issues that arise from trauma. Childhood trauma can steadily turn into ASD if left untreated for a prolonged period. It can be a violent incident, a horrifying accident, or the unexpected death of a loved one. Signs related to traumatization must be recognized at an early stage as teens are at a higher risk of committing suicide or hurting themselves.

## Suicide History

If your family has a history of suicide, your teen may be at risk. The situation can be specifically intense if your child has witnessed someone committing suicide. Whether it's deliberate self-harm or a suicidal attempt, the young minds are easily influenced and vulnerable to committing suicide themselves. Since they are looking for an easy way to solve their issues, harming themselves becomes an easier option if they've witnessed a similar phenomenon. Instead of understanding the real cause and the severity of the situation, they take this intense step without seeking treatment. Several environmental conditions impulsivity also contribute to this condition and increase the chances of familial suicide, which means that both genetic impulses and non-genetic behavioral aspects may be passed on to the next generation. Pay specific attention to your teen's anxiety disorder if your family has been through a similar tragedy.

**Substance Abuse**

As you learned by now, excessive alcohol and drug use can lead to addiction. Since teens are not entirely mature and cannot control the amount of substance they consume, they often cross the line and dwindle into addiction. The use of substances is, directly and indirectly, related to self-destructive behaviors. Substance abuse paired with depression can enhance the intensity of your teen's suicidal mindset and put them in distress until they take a dangerous step. With time, the situation can worsen and lead to suicide. Drugs like lysergic acid diethylamide (LSD) and certain prescribed medications also increase the risk of overdose. In some countries, a lower age limit for drinking also affects teenagers' mindset. In most cases, teens and tweens aged 17 to 20 are more prone to developing suicidal thoughts due to the delicate drinking age limit. Let's not forget how easily teens are influenced by the people around them.

## Signs of Depression

Among all reasons, depression is the number one reason that leads not only teens but also adults into practicing self-destructive behaviors. Depression is linked to anxiety, which can steadily take the suicidal form. Even though the stimulus and effects are not apparent, the coherence can be decoded from the teen's reactions to challenges and circumstances in each step of their life. The fear of failure or not being good enough can trigger depression, and the easiest way to cope is by ending their life. In a few cases, teens have steadily developed symptoms due to the comparison between various classes based on their social status, looks, and popularity. Any painful or demoting emotion is easily translated as the end of one's life, which is why teens lose the meaning of living and resort to self-harm.

## Exposure to Physical or Sexual Violence

Bullying is one form of physical offense that your teen may be exposed to in school or neighborhood. It often boils down to family-related abuse and domestic violence. A teen exposed to violence, directly or indirectly, as a child is highly prone to developing unpleasant thoughts that can lead to self-harm as a coping mechanism. Parents who are imprisoned or have a criminal record also affect the young minds. Even though the parents face some form of violence either from their partner or others, it can majorly affect their children. So, if you live in a violent household, neighborhood, or environment, pay attention to your teen's feelings and emotions as it significantly heightens their anxiety.

## Issues with Sexual Orientation

If a teen cannot accept their sexual orientation or is too scared to open up to their parents and family members, they can be at risk of committing suicide. The fear of being judged by society and not being accepted by others is at the brink of most homosexual teenagers' minds. This phenomenon is widely known as sexual orientation discordance, which elevates the chances of conducting self-harm. However, parents must try to come to terms with their child's mindsets and be open about their choices. After all, it's your child who has to live their life, then why not be happy for them? Since it is arduous and confusing for teens to make peace with their sexual orientation, be more supportive and help them face their emotions instead of making it more difficult.

## What to Look for in a Suicidal Teenager

The best way to save your teenager from committing suicide is to look for signs and taking immediate and effective steps to curtail them.

### Constant Mood Swings

While teens commonly experience occasional mood swings, a consistent pattern can threaten their mental health. Rapid shifts in mood are also connected to severe issues, such as bipolar disorder, which can increase suicidal tendencies. While being happy or sad at occasional intervals is acceptable, it should be taken seriously if it interferes with their lifestyle quality. If your teen is portraying signs of mood swings that seem difficult to control, seek help from professionals to get to the bottom of the issue. In most cases, substance abuse and hormonal changes are the two common causes. However, being extremely happy one day and lashing out at others on the next can take a toll on your teen's mental health. If you see your teen spending a lot of money when they are happy and feel like harming themselves when they are in a bad mood, these are signs of mood swings that can lead to suicide.

## Feeling Hopeless

If your teen is displaying signs of hopelessness and unable to perceive a future, they are also at a higher risk. Feeling hopeless is often related to a chemical imbalance that is difficult to diagnose at an early stage. When combined with the feeling of not being appreciated by their loved ones or rejected by their crush can enhance the emotion of despair they are already facing. The angst is also often shadowed by humiliation and shame. Repetition in behavior, seeking perfection to cover up their guilt, and feeling hopeless or hesitant speech are often accompanying signs.

## Making Suicidal Statements

Statements like "I feel like dying," "I wish to end my life," or "Death seems to be the easiest answer to all these problems" are some direct verbal cues that clearly state a teen's motive. They may even be seen carrying or holding dangerous objects or looking for strategies to harm themselves. It is believed that most teens who constantly make suicidal statements are crying for help. It may seem that your teen is threatening you by narrating instances and statements related to suicide, but it can be much more serious and intimidating than you imagine. Most parents ignore these statements considering them to be attention-seeking. Do not make the same mistake as the adolescents who fail to get help and are often subjects of suicide.

## Staying Isolated

Teenagers who prefer to be alone can steadily develop the mindset of harming themselves. Even if their loved ones are trying to reach them, they somehow feel that they are and will remain alone for the rest of their lives, and this makes the act of committing suicide easier. When they are alone, the risk of self-harm increases as there is no one to monitor or stop them, which is why parents must be more careful when their teens prefer to stay alone most of the time. It is known that loneliness and social isolation are as dangerous as smoking 15 cigarettes a day. Along with cognitive decline, rising physical and mental health issues, impaired immunity, and lack of sleep, most teenagers exposed to suicidal ideation are compelled to harm themselves.

## Previous Attempts at Self-Harm

Teens who have tried to harm themselves in the past are undeniably at a higher risk of taking their lives. Parents must closely monitor their condition and pay attention to their behavioral pattern at all stages. However, just because they have displayed a previous attempt at suicide does not mean that the risk of reattempt will increase. If your teen is provided optimum attention and care, the symptoms can be treated with time. For instance, a simple intervention program held by the guardian or an expert will gain insights into the teen's chances of reattempting suicide.

## Changes in Personality and Attitude

This also often stems from the symptoms and aftereffects of depression. Teens and tweens suffering from depression will be caught portraying changes in their personality and behavior. They may either seem quieter or become meaner. You may even catch them giving away their belongings to others or parting ways with the possessions they valued.

# Diagnosis

## Physical and Mental Health Diagnosis

The first and most important step of diagnosis is noticing and tracking physical and mental health deterioration signs. As mentioned in the previous chapters, individuals with combined signs of physical and mental issues are closely related to the emerging suicide ideation. Blood and urine tests are run to detect physical signs related to hormonal changes and genetic issues. Your teen may also undergo a thorough medical test under a psychiatrist to determine the triggers that compelled them to cause self-harm.

## Type of Medication Prescribed

At times, teens undergoing medication may also get suicidal thoughts, so medical practitioners test the prescriptions and medicines they are taking. Paired with hormonal changes and mood swings, certain over-the-counter drugs are dangerous for young minds. Even though the cases are rare, many teens get suicidal feelings due to the medication they are prescribed.

## Addiction

As mentioned, teens addicted to a varied range of substances are also diagnosed to determine if the substance use was the main cause of fathering their suicidal ideation. The tests will demonstrate if the teen suffered from damages due to alcohol and drug abuse and if they were the main reason behind the suicidal attempt. If they are even borderline addicted, the practitioner will provide medication and therapy to treat it. In extreme cases, they may be sent to a rehabilitation center to cure their addiction.

## Treatment

### Medication

Some medication reduces the signs of suicide and encourages your teen to look at the brighter side. Your teen's medical practitioner will prescribe antipsychotic medications, antidepressants, or medicines related to treat anti-anxiety, depending on their case.

### Psychotherapy

This is probably the most effective way to treat suicide. Commonly known as talk therapy or psychological counseling, this form of treatment will dig deeper into your teen's emotions and help them cope with their fears. It also helps treat and diminish suicidal ideation.

## How Can I Help Prevent Teen Suicide?

As we know, prevention is better than cure in all cases. Instead of treating and amending your teen's suicidal or self-harm, it is best to prevent it from happening in the first place. Failing to pay attention to your teen can push them in the wrong direction and elevate the chances of causing self-harm.

### Reach Out to Your Teen

Instead of giving unwanted and undue criticism, listen to them with an open mind and ask if you can do anything to help. Be with them and mean it. Acknowledge their skills, presence, and talent. Tell them how capable they are of achieving anything they wish. Reach out for help and keep them hooked. In other words, make them feel appreciated.

### Help Them Live a Healthy Lifestyle

Developing a healthy lifestyle by exercising and following a healthy diet are effective strategies to cope with mental health issues and reduce suicidal ideation. For this, you must incorporate some form of physical activity in your routines, such as a 30-min walk or attending a spin class. Plan your teen's diet and feed them healthy food to improve their physical and mental health. Take help from a medical practitioner or certified nutritionist to help you plan a diet based on your teen's mental health condition.

## Keep Alcohol and Harmful Substances out of Reach

Needless to say, keep alcohol, drugs, and other addictive substances out of your teen's reach. They will be tempted to try out every kind of substance that is within their reach. Explain the negative repercussions of drinking alcohol and doing drugs to keep your teen away from such vices, preventing drug overdose or alcohol poisoning suicide. Since young adults are highly likely to commit suicide by popping multiple sleeping pills, ensure that they are kept away from such dangerous triggers.

## Spend More Time with Them

The idea is to show your support as a parent and ward off the negative effects of social isolation. By spending time with them, they will be assured of having someone by their side who will listen and support them. Perform activities that your teen likes to do. Whether it's playing video games, shopping, or baking, do what they like when spending time with them. It keeps them distracted and happy. More importantly, they will feel like sharing their worries and fears with you as you get closer. Staying aligned with a teenager's mind is challenging, especially for parents, and encouraging them to spend time with you is the easiest way to break this barrier.

## Support Them throughout Therapy

At times, just being with them can make a world of difference. Accompany your teen to their therapy sessions and ensure that they are comfortable throughout. Drive them to and from their sessions, especially if they are feeling nervous. If they cannot keep up, talk to their therapist to change their treatment and medication course.

## When to Call a Doctor and How to Handle an Appointment

Even though you took preventive measures and paid attention to your teen, they may still end up harming themselves or attempting suicide. In an emergency, call your partner, family member, or someone close to you to get additional help, and, most importantly, call an emergency service. If you find out that your teen has already attempted suicide and is in a severe condition, call an emergency ambulance service and transfer them to a medical facility at the earliest. Make sure that they are tended to at the earliest to decrease the severity of their condition. The medical practitioner will conduct a thorough examination and look for physical signs of damage in your teen. They will also check for signs to decipher the causes that led your teen to commit suicide. Furthermore, they will also ask you questions related to your teen's previous suicide attempt, if any.

Depending on the severity of the case, your child will be admitted to the hospital to gain further treatment. You will remain at the hospital to supervise your child's condition to avoid a reattempt suicide. Do not feel hesitant to ask questions like, "Are you having thoughts of harming yourself?" and "Are you thinking of committing suicide?" They may sound extremely straightforward and downright pathological, but they help you figure out the severity of the situation. If your teen answers with a yes, immediately take help from the experts. While booking a doctor's appointment may take some time, in the meanwhile, get in touch with a crisis hotline. Most countries have urgent care clinics that take care of patients who have made suicidal attempts.

Lastly, be wary of the misconceptions related to anxiety and suicide. Since most people believe that suicide is solely based on personal decisions, the situation isn't taken as seriously as it should be. Furthermore, statements like, "There is no way out for people with suicidal thoughts" or "You should not talk with people about suicide as it can give them the idea" are completely wrong. In contrast, suicidal impulses are treatable if recognized early. Do not assume that by not talking about suicide, your teen will be safe and avoid causing self-harm.

**Key Takeaway:** Irrespective of how hopeless and worthless your teen might feel, proper attention and care will help them lead a healthy life both physically and mentally. Several cases of teens with suicidal intentions who now lead healthier lives are present today as proof. As a parent, your role is to recognize these tendencies and pull your teen out of danger at the earliest.

# CHAPTER 10:

# PARENTING AND ANXIETY

When dealing with your teens' anxiety, you must be prepared to keep up and pull your teen out of this misery. As instructed on an airplane to wear oxygen masks before assisting others, consider a similar situation when helping your anxious teen. This chapter will take a look at some self-care tips for parents and how to deal with your anxiety to help your child in a better way.

## Self-Care Tips for Parents

Consider these self-care tips for parents to control anxiety and take care of themselves to help their teens in despair.

## Start Prioritizing

Prioritize your needs and tasks to stay on track and understand what is important and what can be discarded. It will also help you organize your schedule and map out your tasks based on your week. Parents are not superheroes who can work continuously without becoming exhausted. You are a human and get tired after working for long hours. Create a work-life balance by prioritizing your tasks and setting your obligations apart. Most of the time, priorities include spending time with your loved ones and family members. Share your priorities that seem like an obligation with your partner, making them easier to handle. With your partner's help, you can make difficult decisions with ease and fulfill them in a jiffy. Note that your priorities aren't your tasks, so they should not be perceived or treated as milestones or things on your to-do list. Your tasks that cannot be deemed as priorities should be taken off the list.

## Take Some Time Out

As parents, you should take some time out for yourselves to rejuvenate and feel fresh. Working all week and fulfilling your duties takes a major toll on your physical and mental health. By taking some time out for yourself, you will take better care of your health and supervise your teen's condition with optimum diligence. Even if you cannot take an entire day or week off due to your busy schedule, take at least 20 to 30 minutes off in a day, preferably before bed. Use this time to relax, distress, and do what you love - read a book, lie down while listening to music, confront your thoughts, and get your head clear.

## Spending Time with Your Loved Ones

Spend time with your children, partner, family members, and those you consider close every once in a while. Since humans are swamped in daily chores and obligations, they often forget to interact with others. Structure your time so that you see and spend time with your loved ones and your family. It is not only necessary for you as parents but also for your teenager. Host dinners and organize informal parties for your loved ones to stay in touch with each other. You can also organize a routine or design a ritual to spend time with your family after dinner. After dinner, playing a board game is a simple ritual that goes a long way in keeping your family united and close. Plan a game night with your loved ones or take cooking classes with your teen. Take your family out on a camping trip or hiking in nature, which helps treat your family's mental health issues, too.

**Pamper Yourself**

You have all the right to pamper yourself, and you completely deserve it. Do not feel guilty when taking a break and indulging in your favorite activities. Take a nap, read your favorite book, sip on a warm cup of tea, and light a scented candle. At times, simple pleasures like these can go a long way and make you appreciate life. Indulge in mindfulness practices, such as visiting a spa or taking a break and watching movies at home. Whether you have 10 minutes or an entire day, you can find ways to pamper yourself at home. For instance, if you have just 10 to 15 minutes to spare, wear a facial mask and meditate while listening to calming music. On the contrary, if you have the whole day free, take a nap, visit your favorite restaurant, or run a movie marathon.

**Find Your Support System**

While you need to take care of yourself to supervise your teen's condition, it's important to find yourself a caretaker or support system to lean on. You need your own caretaker to share your worries with and who can provide optimum assistance in times of despair. Even though you might have several people in your life, narrow down your options by considering the people who will help you in times of need. It can be your parents, best friend, or a well-wisher who will carefully listen to your thoughts and help you overcome them. Is there anyone you respect and go to for advice in distressing times? Sometimes, you don't want someone to listen but just be there for you and provide comfort as you face your fears.

**Go Out**

Whenever you get time, go out and celebrate the tiny milestones in your life. Whether it's going to a diner to grab a milkshake or going on a long road trip with your family, go out as much as you can. It will keep you excited and on your toes. Do not consider grocery shopping or running errands as going out. Be out in nature, go for a walk, or take your children to an amusement park. Spending time outside with your family will help you rekindle decaying relationships and reconstruct a new bond.

## Organization Matters

While organizing your life and prioritizing your needs is of the utmost importance, also ensure that the environment you live in is organized. Being and living in a cluttered space is extremely off-putting and causes stress. It also makes finding essential things on time a lot more difficult. When decluttering your space, start by collecting and discarding things you don't use or won't use in the future. Do not get emotionally attached to your belongings. Let them go and give them away to people in need. With a clear space and environment, you will think clearly, too. For some people, cleaning and decluttering is a form of therapy. Try it for yourself, and you will feel at ease, too. If it seems too overwhelming, ask your family to help and turn it into a fun family activity.

By organization, we also mean organizing various other factors of your life. For instance, it can be managing your expenses and finances, scheduling time to prepare your meals and spend time with your family, and organizing your time to indulge in a self-care routine. Failing to organize your life will not only delay your chores but also keep you super busy. In such cases, forget about pampering yourself or taking time out to relax.

## Concentrate On Your Future

Instead of cribbing about your past, divert all your attention towards making a better future. Whether it's the next day or the next five years, draft a rough idea to keep your goals in mind. If your main goal needs a lot of hard work and capital, start working on it today and saving money.

## Your Health is Important

If you are unhealthy and keep getting sick, there is no hope for your child to stay robust. After all, you have to take care of their melancholy and treat it at the earliest. If you, the support system, fall ill, there is no one to take care of your teen. So, keep your health in check, making it a priority. Take care of your physical, mental, and emotional health as all three are necessary to stay active and think straight. A slight imbalance in this system can create havoc and worsen the situation.

Here is how you can take care of your physical health.

**Exercise Regularly:** Join a gym or take a spin class to keep your body in shape. Exercising helps you lose weight, maintains your physical health, and keeps your mental health in check. Since exercising is also known to balance your hormonal levels and secrete endorphins (the happy hormone), you will feel much more active and productive throughout the day. Encourage your teen and other family members to participate in some form of physical activity with you. Even if you cannot take some time out to exercise due to a busy schedule, try to squeeze in at least 30 minutes of walking throughout the day.

**Design a Well-Balanced and Nutritious Diet**: A balanced and nutritious diet is essential to provide the necessary nutrients to your body for optimum functioning and health. It will also help treat any existing health issues and prevent other problems from occurring. For instance, the risk of strokes, diabetes, osteoporosis, and some cancers can be lowered by designing a nutritious diet. Do not take the risk of designing a diet on your own. Consult a certified nutritionist to help you prepare a food chart based on your existing physical and health condition.

**Drink Plenty of Water:** Drink at least 8 to 10 glasses of water in a day. This is the minimum amount per day but the more, the better. It reduces stress levels and keeps you hydrated. Dehydration is the main cause of several health issues, such as migraine and kidney problems, so drinking more water keeps such issues at bay. Keep a water bottle or jug on your table to remind you to keep sipping on water throughout the day. You can also make lemonade or drink hot tea to complete your daily water intake.

**Get 8 Hours of Sleep**: Sleep is the solution to many health problems. Getting less sleep will not only affect your eyes and skin but also increase your stress levels. Lack of sleep can lead to drastic weight gain in a shorter period. Sleep and anxiety are closely interlinked, so you should focus on getting at least 7 to 8 hours of sound sleep every night. If you have trouble falling asleep, sip on chamomile tea and listen to peaceful music before going to bed. Once you train your body to sleep and wake up at a designated time, its circadian rhythms will adjust accordingly and help you sleep at the same time each night.

Here are some mindfulness practices to include in your regimen to improve your mental health and ward off your anxiety.

**Visualization Techniques**: These self-imagery techniques are known to treat anxiety, agoraphobia, and panic attacks due to their ability to calm your mind. They also help you get in touch with your true and unfiltered emotions, which eventually reduce anxiety symptoms and related disorders. One of the most effective ways to practice visualization techniques is by tuning into guided imagery. Close your eyes and lie down on a flat surface. Play calming music to concentrate and place your hands beside you. Imagine any scene or place that you love. It could be a beach, the woods, or the mountains. Take deep breaths and imagine being there as you slowly guide your imagination to explore the virtual place. Once you are fully immersed in your imagination, slowly open your eyes and notice how your mind and body feel. Practice this exercise daily, preferably when you feel super anxious.

**Breathing Techniques**: Since your breathing is often affected by anxiety, practice certain breathing exercises to alleviate the symptoms. This technique is super helpful during anxiety attacks and rapid breathing. While deep breathing and meditation help, you can also try abdomen and belly breathing techniques to feel calmer. Your one hand should rest on your chest and the other on your abdomen or belly. Inhale deeply and notice your belly rising as the air enters your body. Keep your stomach muscles engaged when exhaling through your mouth. Try resonate breathing or alternate nostril breathing techniques for a similar effect.

**Journaling**: Keep a diary or a journal and enlist your feelings and thoughts that you go through all day. Since journaling is an effective stress-buster and helps you cope with your fears, it is a sure-shot way to combat anxiety. It is also great for overall wellbeing and improving your emotional health. You can unleash your creativity and go limitless with how you journal. Use stickers, colorful pens, or any other creative tools to make journaling an enjoyable experience and a hobby you'd look forward to daily. Keep track of your eating habits, exercise regime, and any other tasks when journaling to improve your wellbeing.

Another way to feel at ease is by practicing gratitude every night before you go to bed. Mention three things you are grateful for and write them down in your diary. It can be anything as lucid as the food on your plate or as magnificent as your huge house. This might seem useless, but it does work in the long run. Knowing that you have something to be thankful for, you will feel happier and blessed, which means a great deal to your mental health.

With these practices, you can keep your senses in check and eliminate the chances of getting caught up in a loop of anxious thoughts, worries, and fears.

## Get Yourself Checked

Schedule regular appointments at your doctor's clinic and get yourself checked every once in a while. Whether it's your general practitioner or your dentist, take care of your body and be aware of it by getting yourself checked once every 6 months. If needed, get your blood and urine tests to treat your nutrient deficiency and design a healthier diet.

Whether or not you suffer from anxiety or a related disorder, consider these self-care tips and make them a permanent part of your lifestyle as they will help you feel calmer and create a work-life balance.

## Learn What Triggers You

You cannot treat your teen's anxiety if you fail to control your condition. If you can recognize signs that may seem like an anxiety disorder, get yourself checked and identify the triggers for better control. Instead of dwelling on your anxiety and worries, recognize what created them in the first place. Once you can identify the triggers, you can treat them effectively. By doing this homework, you will help your anxious teen, too. Merely because you feel a certain way does not necessarily mean that you have a serious health issue, so recognize the signs, become aware, and stay in tune with your body.

Once you know your triggers, you can easily set boundaries and keep them away to cope with the situation more sensibly. Learning what triggers you helps you design a treatment plan that effectively combats the situation and reduces symptoms. As mentioned, if you are calm, you can take care of your anxious teen too. While being stressed is a common phenomenon in most adults, it can become an issue if it turns into hypertension or anxiety. Therefore, learn about your triggers at the earliest.

**Know-How to Combat Stress**

Combating and managing stress becomes easier when you know what's causing it. While simple self-care tips are an effective way to cope with stress and feel at ease, suitable steps should be taken to tackle more intense situations. Consult a clinician or a therapist if your stress or anxiety seems unmanageable. Combating your stress is even more necessary as your teen replicates your behavior. If they see you effectively managing your stress and coping with your anxiety, they will model your behavior and take cues from you. This simultaneous process can efficiently scaffold your teen's way of managing stress and tolerating anxiety.

The breathing and mindfulness practices described above help alleviate anxiety and panic. If your situation seems intense, seek help from a medical practitioner and recognize your triggers to treat them more effectively. Once you know how to tolerate and ward off stress, teach your teen the same mannerisms and encourage them to take cues. The modeling behavior of children that we mentioned in previous chapters can help here. If your idea is to rationally think when feeling anxious, convey the same feeling and ask your teen relevant questions. For instance, calm your teen by conveying the exact emotions you feel when dealing with anxiety. A statement like, "Being scared is not uncommon, but what are the chances that you will face something so scary?" This can significantly help your child cope with their issue and feel calmer. Whether or not you are coping with your anxiety, always stay calm and composed in front of your child. Since your teens will model your behavior, your words, how you express your emotions, and the intensity of your facial expressions, you must be extra careful.

**Key Takeaway**: Before you learn about and treat your teen's anxiety, it is necessary to treat your anxiety disorder or any other form of mental illness first. It helps you cope with your child's condition and pull them out of this hole at the earliest. Once you can identify the triggers, take the necessary steps to treat them and alleviate anxiety. Consider the self-care tips taught in this chapter to create a work-life balance and cope with your anxiety. Spend some time out, do things you like, and take care of your health to build a strong support system and backbone for your teen.

# **CONCLUSION**

While you may wish to turn back time and prevent the problem from occurring in the first place, we all know it is not impossible. The only thing you can do is look ahead and find a solution by digging deeper into the crux of the problem. Instead of cursing your younger self, look out for your teen and help them cope with their issues.

As mentioned throughout the book, treating chronic anxiety is extremely crucial, especially in teens, as it can deteriorate their quality of life and become a life-threatening episode.

Let's summarize what we've learned so far to illustrate an overall picture. Start by understanding what anxiety is and whether or not it is normal. Since anxiety is more frequently detected in adults, teens and tweens' anxiety can seem overwhelming for parents. However, instead of panicking, understand if your teen actually has chronic anxiety. Next, narrow down the plausible causes that could have led to the moments of panic that your teen regularly goes through. At times, peer pressure, changing hormones, rising competition, and societal pressure are the main reasons. In other cases, parents unknowingly push their kids into a downward spiral that steadily gives birth to anxious thoughts.

Garner help from this book to recognize the exact signs and causes of teenage anxiety. Some effective treatment options based on your child's condition and the circumstance's severity are also mentioned. Next, know how to talk to your kid about anxiety and what not to say. Saying the wrong thing can trigger negative feelings and worsen the condition. Refer to the examples of phrases and statements mentioned in chapter 6 to put your child at ease. Assure your teen that you're with them and acting as a support system 24/7.

Deploy effective strategies to combat the situation, support your teen, and portray your expectations. You can also teach self-soothing techniques such as deep breathing, aerobic exercises, and mindfulness practices to ease the symptoms. If your teen has already been clinically diagnosed with chronic anxiety, keep an eye on them to prevent the development of suicidal ideation. Closely monitor the situation if they have previously attempted suicide or have harmed themselves. Lastly, do not forget to take care of yourself. After all, your child needs a strong support system.

The next step is to take action. Now that you have all the information you need, start applying it and help your child overcome their anxiety. The sooner you begin, the easier it will be to solve their problems. Since young minds are unaware of how to handle and deal with unfavorable situations, you have to step in and alleviate the symptoms as their guardian.

Finally, if you found the book useful and wish other parents to gain insights on treating their child's anxiety, leave a review for this book to reach as many parents as possible.

# REFERENCES

6 hidden signs of teen anxiety. (n.d.). Retrieved from Psycom.net website: https://www.psycom.net/hidden-signs-teen-anxiety/

6 things you should never say to teens with anxiety disorders. (2016, October 5). Retrieved from Discoverymood.com website: https://discoverymood.com/blog/6-things-never-say-teens-anxiety-disorders/

10 things never to say to your anxious child. (n.d.). Retrieved from Psycom.net website: https://www.psycom.net/child-anxiety-things-never-to-say

Amy Morin, L. (n.d.). How to help a shy teen build self-confidence. Retrieved from Verywellfamily.com website: https://www.verywellfamily.com/how-to-help-a-shy-teen-build-self-confidence-2611009

Ankrom, S., MS, & LCPC. (n.d.). The difference between fear and anxiety. Retrieved from Verywellmind.com website: https://www.verywellmind.com/fear-and-anxiety-differences-and-similarities-2584399

Anxiety in teens - how to help a teenager deal with anxiety - hey Sigmund. (2016, October 21). Retrieved from Heysigmund.com website: https://www.heysigmund.com/anxiety-in-teens/

Anxiety in Teens is Rising: What's Going On? (n.d.). Retrieved from Healthychildren.org website: https://www.healthychildren.org/English/health-issues/conditions/emotional-problems/Pages/Anxiety-Disorders.aspx

Can gastric disorders contribute to Anxiety and Depression? (n.d.). Retrieved from Mentalhelp.net website: https://www.mentalhelp.net/blogs/can-gastric-disorders-contribute-to-anxiety-and-depression/

Cho, J. (2016, June 1). 13 things about social anxiety disorder you may not have known. Forbes Magazine. Retrieved from https://www.forbes.com/sites/jeenacho/2016/06/01/13-things-about-social-anxiety-disorder-you-may-not-have-known/

Helping your anxious child or teen. (n.d.). Retrieved from Heretohelp.bc.ca website: https://www.heretohelp.bc.ca/infosheet/helping-your-anxious-child-or-teen

Holland, K. (2018, September 19). Anxiety: Causes, symptoms, treatment, and more. Retrieved from Healthline.com website: https://www.healthline.com/health/anxiety

Managing and treating anxiety. (n.d.). Retrieved from Gov.au website: https://www.betterhealth.vic.gov.au/health/conditionsandtreatments/anxiety-treatment-options

Matheis, L. (n.d.). The do's and don'ts of parenting an anxious teen. Psychology Today. Retrieved from https://www.psychologytoday.com/blog/special-matters/201904/the-dos-and-don-ts-parenting-anxious-teen

Meyerowitz, A. (2018, June 6). 13 physical symptoms you didn't know were caused by anxiety. Retrieved from Redonline.co.uk website: https://www.redonline.co.uk/health-self/self/a528103/13-physical-symptoms-you-didnt-know-were-caused-by-anxiety/

Mindfulness – is it for you? (n.d.). Retrieved from Reachout.com website: https://au.reachout.com/articles/mindfulness-is-it-for-you

Morgan, K. (n.d.). How anxiety affects your focus. BBC. Retrieved from https://www.bbc.com/worklife/article/20200611-how-anxiety-affects-your-focus

Northwestern Medicine. (n.d.). The impact of unspoken peer pressure. Retrieved from Www.nm.org website: https://www.nm.org/healthbeat/healthy-tips/emotional-health/unspoken-peer-pressure

O'Grady, S. J. (2018, August 30). Social anxiety disorder: When fear leads to isolation. Retrieved from Webmd.com website: https://blogs.webmd.com/mental-health/20180830/social-anxiety-disorder-when-fear-leads-to-isolation

ReachOut Australia. (2020, October 14). What is anxiety? Retrieved from Reachout.com website: https://au.reachout.com/articles/what-is-anxiety

Spector, N. (2019, May 20). A mental health check-in: 14 questions to ask your child. Retrieved from NBC News website: https://www.nbcnews.com/better/lifestyle/mental-health-check-14-questions-ask-your-child-ncna1006936

Teen depression and anxiety: What parents can do to help. (2018, October 13). Retrieved from Lynnlyons.com website: https://www.lynnlyons.com/teen-depression-anxiety/

Wright, L. W. (2019, September 17). Signs of anxiety in tweens and teens. Retrieved from Understood.org website: https://www.understood.org/en/friends-feelings/managing-feelings/stress-anxiety/signs-your-teen-or-tween-is-struggling-with-anxiety

(N.d.-a). Retrieved from Adaa.org website: https://adaa.org/understanding-anxiety

(N.d.-b). Retrieved from Apa.org website: https://www.apa.org/monitor/2013/07-08/dull-moment

5 ways to deal with anxiety. (n.d.). Retrieved from Kidshealth.org website: https://kidshealth.org/en/teens/anxiety-tips.html

6 hidden signs of teen anxiety. (n.d.). Retrieved from Psycom.net website: https://www.psycom.net/hidden-signs-teen-anxiety/

Anxiety in teenagers. (2020, July 17). Retrieved from Net.au website: https://raisingchildren.net.au/pre-teens/mental-health-physical-health/stress-anxiety-depression/anxiety

Anxiety medications for teens: Treatment options for your child. (n.d.). Retrieved from Psycom.net website: https://www.psycom.net/anxiety-medications-teenagers

Cherney, K. (2014, September 24). Effects of anxiety on the body. Retrieved from Healthline.com website: https://www.healthline.com/health/anxiety/effects-on-body

Common Causes of Anxiety in Teens and Young Adults. (2020, May 26). Retrieved from Paradigmtreatment.com website: https://paradigmtreatment.com/anxiety-teens-young-adults/common-causes/

Villiers, D. (2020, April 24). Is my child's anxiety "normal"? Retrieved from Anxietyinstitute.com website: https://anxietyinstitute.com/is-my-childs-anxiety-normal/

Anxiety in teenagers. (2020, July 17). Raising Children Network. https://raisingchildren.net.au/pre-teens/mental-health-physical-health/stress-anxiety-depres-sion/anxiety#:%7E:text=If%20your%20teenage%20child%20is,giving%20a%20presentation%20in%20class.

Banes, K. (2016, April 1). 6 ways good parents contribute to their child's anxiety. Washington Post.
https://www.washingtonpost.com/news/parenting/wp/2016/04/01/6-ways-good-parents-contribute-to-their-childs-anxiety/

Doyle, K. (2013, December 13). Parent behaviors linked to kids' anxiety, depression. U.S. https://www.reuters.com/article/us-parent-kids-anxiety-depression-idUSBRE9BC0VR20131213

Li, P. (2021, March 25). Controlling Parents – The Signs And Why They Are Harmful. Parenting For Brain.
https://www.parentingforbrain.com/controlling-parents/

Lindberg, S. L. (2020, September 25). Bad Parenting: Signs, Effects, and How to Change It. Healthline.
https://www.healthline.com/health/parenting/bad-parenting#signs

Walton, A. G. (2012, August 3). How Parents' Stress Can Hurt A Child, From The Inside Out. Forbes.
https://www.forbes.com/sites/alicegwalton/2012/07/25/how-parents-stress-can-hurt-a-child-from-the-inside-out/?sh=2d87260f6b38

Building a Crisis Kit. (2020, September 28). The Recovery Village Drug and Alcohol Rehab.
https://www.therecoveryvillage.com/mental-health/related/crisis-kits/

Halloran, J. (2021, January 9). Coping Skill Spotlight: 5 4 3 2 1 Grounding Technique. Coping Skills for Kids.
https://copingskillsforkids.com/blog/2016/4/27/coping-skill-spotlight-5-4-3-2-1-grounding-technique

Helping someone with anxiety and panic attacks. (n.d.). Mind. https://www.mind.org.uk/information-support/types-of-mental-health-problems/anxiety-and-panic-attacks/for-friends-and-family/

How to Help Someone with Anxiety. (n.d.). Johns Hopkins Medicine. https://www.hopkinsmedicine.org/health/treatment-tests-and-therapies/how-to-help-someone-with-anxiety

Reframe Anxiety Thoughts. (n.d.). Yahoo. https://www.yahoo.com/lifestyle/reframe-anxiety-thoughts-now-using-111522096.html

Why worrying isn't always a bad thing. (2013, January 13). Independent. https://www.independent.ie/regionals/herald/lifestyle/health-beauty/why-worrying-isnt-always-a-bad-thing-27980020.html

Young, K. (2020, August 7). Anxiety in Teens – How to Help a Teenager Deal With Anxiety. Hey Sigmund. https://www.heysigmund.com/anxiety-in-teens/

Schab, L., 2008. The anxiety workbook for teens. Oakland, CA: Instant Help Books.

Chambala, A. (2008). Anxiety and Art Therapy: Treatment in the Public Eye. Art Therapy, 25(4), 187-189.

Ankrom, S. (2021). Deep Breathing Exercises to Reduce Anxiety. Retrieved from https://www.verywellmind.com/abdominal-breathing-2584115

Schab, L. (2008). Anxiety Workbook for Teens. [Place of publication not identified]: New Harbinger Publications.

Vick, R. (1999). Utilizing Prestructured Art Elements in Brief Group Art Therapy with Adolescents. Art Therapy, 16(2), 68-77.

Amy Morin, L. (n.d.). 15 Self-Care Strategies for Parents. Retrieved from Verywellfamily.com website: https://www.verywellfamily.com/self-care-for-parents-4178010

Burton, N. (2020, November 2). Self-care strategies for parents when you have no time for yourself. Retrieved from Healthline.com website: https://www.healthline.com/health/parenting/self-care-strategies-for-parents-no-time

Gene Beresin, Executive Director, & Braaten, E. (2020, January 8). 10 self-care tips for parents. Retrieved from Mghclaycenter.org website: https://www.mghclaycenter.org/parenting-concerns/10-self-care-tips-for-parents/

Parents passing anxiety to children. (2016, February 23). Retrieved from Childmind.org website: https://childmind.org/article/how-to-avoid-passing-anxiety-on-to-your-kids/

Self-care and support for parents and caregivers of young children (14). (n.d.). Retrieved from Gov.au website: https://www.betterhealth.vic.gov.au/health/HealthyLiving/self-care-support-for-parents-caregiver-14

www.ingramcontent.com/pod-product-compliance
Lightning Source LLC
Chambersburg PA
CBHW071414070526
44578CB00003B/579